A TRAVEL GUIDE TO

Renaissance
Florence

Other books in the Travel Guide series:

A TRAVEL GUIDE TO

Renaissance
Florence

James Barter

**LUCENT
BOOKS**

THOMSON
™
GALE

San Diego • Detroit • New York • San Francisco • Cleveland • New Haven, Conn. • Waterville, Maine • London • Munich

THOMSON

✷

GALE

© 2003 by Lucent Books. Lucent Books is an imprint of The Gale Group, Inc.,
a division of Thomson Learning, Inc.

Lucent Books® and Thomson Learning™ are trademarks used herein under license.

For more information, contact
Lucent Books
27500 Drake Rd.
Farmington Hills, MI 48331-3535
Or you can visit our Internet site at http://www.gale.com

LIBRARY OF CONGRESS CATALOGING-IN-PUBLICATION DATA

Barter, James, 1946–
    Renaissance Florence / by James Barter.
        p. cm. — (A travel guide to:)
    Includes bibliographical references and index.
    Summary: Examines the history, people, educational system, scientific and artistic
    discoveries, social structure, shopping, festivals, and famous artists of Florence.
        ISBN 1-59018-145-X (lib. : alk. paper)
        1. Florence (Italy)—Guidebooks—Juvenile literature. [1. Florence (Italy) 2. Italy.] I.
    Title. II. Series.
        DG732 .B34 2003
        914.4'510484—dc21
                                                            2001006816

Printed in the United States of America

Contents

FOREWORD

Travel can be a unique way to learn about oneself and other cultures. The esteemed American writer and historian, John Hope Franklin, poetically expressed his conviction in the value of travel by urging, "We must go beyond textbooks, go out into the bypaths and untrodden depths of the wilderness and travel and explore and tell the world the glories of our journey." The message communicated by this eloquent entreaty is clear: The value of travel is to temper one's imagination about a place and its people with reality, and instead of thinking how things may be, to be able to experience them as they really are.

Franklin's voice is not alone in his summons for students to "travel and explore." He is joined by a stentorian chorus of thinkers that includes former president John F. Kennedy, who established the Peace Corps to facilitate cross-cultural understandings between Americans and citizens of other lands. Ideas about the benefits of travel do not spring only from contemporary times. The ancient Greek historian, Herodotus, journeyed to foreign lands for the purpose of immersing himself in unfamiliar cultural traditions. In this way, he believed, he might gain a firsthand understanding of people and ways of life in other places.

The joys, insights, and satisfaction that travelers derive from their journeys are not limited to cultural understanding. Travel has the added value of enhancing the traveler's inner self by expanding his or her range of experiences. Writer Paul Tournier concurs that, "The real meaning of travel, like that of a conversation by the fireside, is the discovery of oneself through contact with other people."

The Lucent Books' Travel Guide, series enlivens history by introducing a new and innovative style and format. Each volume in the series presents the history of a preeminent historical travel destination written in the casual style and format of a travel guide. Whether providing a tour of fifth-century Athens, Renaissance Florence, or Shakespeare's London, each book describes a city or area at its cultural peak and orients readers to only those places and activities that are known to have existed at that time.

A high level of authenticity is achieved in the Travel Guide series. Each book is written in the present tense and addresses the reader as a prospective foreign traveler. The sense of authenticity is further achieved, whenever possible, by the inclusion of descriptive quotations by contemporary writers who knew the place; information on fascinating historical sites; and travel tips meant to explain unusual cultural idiosyncrasies that give depth and texture to all great cultural centers. Even shopping details, such as where to buy an ermine trimmed gown, or a much-needed house slave are included to inform readers of what items were sought after throughout history.

Looked at collectively, this series presents an appealing presentation of many of the cultural and social highlights of Western civilization. The collection also provides a framework for discussion about the larger historical currents that dominated not only each travel destination but countries and entire continents as well. Each book is customized by the author to bring to the fore the most important and most interesting characteristics that define each title. High standards of scholarship are assured in the series by the generous peppering of relevant quotes and extensive bibliographies. These tools provide readers a scholastic standard for their own research as well as a guide to direct them to other books, periodicals, and websites that will provide them greater breadth and detail.

The Flower of Italy

T his is an exciting time in *Firenze*, the city known as the Flower of Italy. The year is 1512 and Florence is celebrating its liberation from attack by French forces. Florentines are also celebrating the return of their most prominent family, the Medici, who had ruled the city for several generations before their exile in 1494.

In addition to the usual political squabbles, considerable internal turmoil had led to conflict between the city's most powerful and wealthy families. Fueling this conflict were two ene-

A panoramic view of Florence, a city known for its stunning architecture, talented artists, and joyous festivities.

mies of the Medici. One, a monk by the name of Girolamo Savonarola, was executed for heresy in 1498. The other, a statesman and writer critical of the Medici family, Niccolò Machiavelli, was exiled. The elimination of these two firebrands has restored social calm to the city.

All Florentines now look forward to a return of the prosperity and rich cultural tradition that had made Florence the most beautiful as well as the most famous city for art in all of Europe. At this time, the city anticipates the return of tourists and visitors eager to view the latest art treasures produced by three of Florence's most respected contemporary artists, Leonardo da Vinci, Michelangelo, and the talented young painter, Raphael. In addition, the old architectural treasures such as Giotto's bell tower, the Baptistery, and the cathedral's dome by Brunelleschi have been cleaned and their marble exteriors sparkle in the Tuscan sun.

The city is now more beautiful and safer than ever for visitors. This travel book has been written to assist everyone wishing to vacation there. It is filled with helpful information about the city's history, how best to get there, places to eat and sleep, and of course, descriptions of the city's fabled art collection and countless shopping opportunities.

CHAPTER ONE

A Brief History of Florence

Visitors wandering the cobblestone streets of modern Florence today, 1512, could not possibly find evidence of the city's origin. The major structures that dominate the city's central district cover any remnants of the earliest peoples who once inhabited this plot of land. Although the origins of the city date back some two thousand years to 500 B.C., finding evidence beyond the stories told by contemporary chroniclers is impossible. Although most people today recognize that the region surrounding Florence, called Tuscany, was once inhabited by a civilization called Etruscan, hence the name Tuscany, no one knows where they came from or if they actually lived on the present site of Florence.

Florence Under the Romans

Far more information, however, is known about Florence under Roman rule. The earliest history of the city known to modern Florentines dates back to the great Roman general and statesman, Julius Caesar. In the year 59 B.C., when Caesar was elected to the Roman consulship—the highest ranking political office in Rome—he ordered the founding of a Roman colony at a point where the Arno River winds its way out of the Tuscan mountains and the river crossing is the easiest. He named the town *Florentia*, a Latin word meaning either "blooming with flowers" or "flourishing town." Nearly all Florentines today accept the former translation because flowers bloom in abundance in the surrounding meadows, and the city's official emblem has always been the lily.

The Roman colony began as a walled military camp that later expanded to include the wives and children of the soldiers and all of the necessary shops and buildings found in any small town. Builders today continue to find the remnants of the aqueduct at the south end of the city, a theater, and even a small coliseum like the one in Rome where gladiators once fought. Florence's biggest church, Santa Maria del Fiore, presently stands on the northwest corner of the camp.

By the second century A.D., during the reign of the emperor Hadrian, all tribes living in northern Italy had been brought into the Roman Empire and Florence began to flourish as a commercial center. Citizens of Rome especially valued the copper pots and woolen goods that Florentine merchants shipped south. The once great forests surrounding Florence were cut down and sold as timber to make way for the orchards and vineyards that still grace the countryside. By this time, the city's population numbered about ten thousand residents and the city was beginning to grow beyond its walls.

At the beginning of the fifth century, Florence experienced tremendous upheaval. The power and influence of

Julius Caesar, depicted here crossing the Rubicon River in northern Italy, gave Florence its name in the first century B.C.

the Roman Empire was showing severe signs of strain. A century earlier, it had been weakened and divided into two separate empires; one in the East that later became the Byzantine Empire and the other in western Europe. Waves of invaders from the north overran and sacked Florence, along with nearly all other Roman cities in the western empire. The fall of the Roman Empire in 476 witnessed the deposition of the last Roman emperor, Romulus Augustus, by the German warlord, Odoacer, who became king of Italy.

The Middle Ages

Florence was now defenseless. Without the power of the Roman legions to protect the city, Florence was hit particularly hard by a tribe from Germany called the Goths. These invaders had been kept at bay behind the Rhine River for generations as their resentment toward Rome's empire mounted. As the invaders spilled across the Rhine into northern Italy on their way to Rome, they found Florence lying directly in their path without protection. The Goths pillaged and then destroyed all of the major buildings in

The Roman Camp

A fortified *castrum* (the Latin word for camp) such as *Florentia* was erected with two primary goals in mind. First, to provide a physical barrier that is large enough for the occupying force to use as a place of operations for subduing the surrounding opposition. Second, that it is strong enough to prevent attackers from breaking in.

When planning a brand new town, Roman civil engineers used the same design and construction standards that they had used on previous camps. The layout was square in shape—*Florentia* was about eight blocks long on each side—surrounded by high stone walls. Entry to the camp was through one of four gates located at the four points of the compass. Two main streets were laid out at right angles to each other, forming an intersection right in the middle of the town. The road running north-south was always named Via Principia (main street), and the one running east-west was always named Via Praetoria (commander street). Both of these streets extended outside the town through the four fortified gates in the outer defensive wall. All secondary streets were also built straight and at right angles to each other.

Using this camp as a base of operations, the Roman soldiers subdued any resistance to their expansion as they pushed north. As the importance of the camp grew and the population increased with wives and children, large public buildings were added within the camp to provide for the needs of the Roman citizens. As such camps expanded, large modern cities such as Florence gradually emerged.

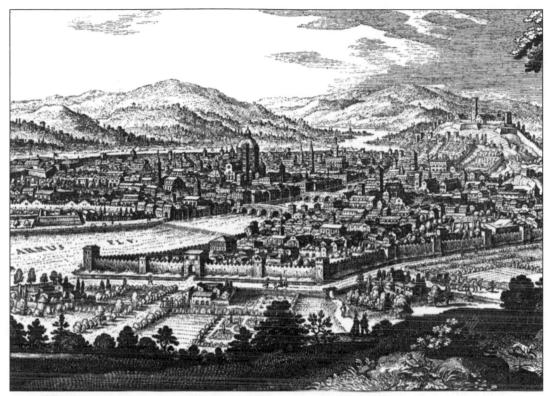

Stone defense towers are evenly spaced in the walls that protect the city.

Florence. The population of the city, reflecting the destruction, plummeted to about one thousand.

Pillaging and warfare became a way of life for many generations and little else is known about ancient Florence until 1078 when a new Florence arose on top of the rubble of the old town. Stone walls once again surrounded the new city but with an entirely new look. Because of continuing fears of invasions, wealthy Florentine families constructed several dozen tall stone defense towers within the city walls that functioned as a second line of defense in case invaders breached the outer walls.

As Florence continued to prosper, its leaders asserted the city's right to self-government by creating an independent republic. The population increased to ten thousand, trading resumed with the neighboring towns, a wealthy merchant class emerged, and the hillside vineyards and orchards filled with the fruit of successful agriculture. The prosperity of the city, however, did not go unnoticed by the Germans. For the next two hundred years, Florence fought one war after another to keep the Germans out of the city's affairs. By 1250, the Germans had tired of the conflict and permanently withdrew from Florence.

Defense Towers

As Florence and other Italian cities expanded, their skylines underwent change as they recognized that their protective walls were not always reliable. For wealthy families, the solution to protection from invasion was the construction of stone towers throughout the city. Although all of the defense towers are now gone, at one time Florence had more than two dozen to protect large families. Sometimes, families in a city would cluster the towers together for mutual protection.

Lacking windows or any stone embellishments, these towers had the rugged look of sentries prepared to do battle. These defense towers, which rose high above the city, had either a square or rectangular base. The doors, usually made of very heavy oak, were studded with iron spikes to prevent enemy axes and saws from cutting through the wood. The roofs were flat so they could be used as an extensive platform from which soldiers could attack invaders down below by dropping heavy stones, throwing down burning twigs, or pouring boiling oil and water on attackers.

Sieges sometimes lasted for months. For this reason, most defense towers were built over water wells and contained storage rooms for dry food and sleeping quarters on the upper levels. Massive and simple, these towers were built to absorb brutal punishment. Catapults could hurl hundred-pound boulders against their walls without breaching them. Attempts to force defenders out by building bonfires around the towers also failed because of their stone construction. In these towers, defenders could signal back and forth with flags and bells to notify other towers about their battle status, food supplies, and strategies to coordinate their defense.

Remarkably resilient, the city's population surged to twenty thousand and Florence began a campaign to take over many of the smaller neighboring cities. The stronger and more prosperous Florentines handily conquered one town after another and by the late thirteenth century, prosperity had swelled the city's population to forty-five thousand, larger than the population of London. The city itself, now fifteen times the size of the original Roman colony, was becoming the envy of Europe. The main streets of the city were now paved in stone, the old stone defense towers were torn down to make way for beautiful churches and municipal buildings, four stone bridges spanned the Arno River that meanders through the city, and wealthy merchants constructed beautiful villas for the enjoyment of their families.

Bankers to the World

As calm returned to northern Italy, life began to return to normal. Trade flourished in coastal cities such as Venice, Genoa, and Pisa where large oceangoing fleets could load and unload their exotic cargos. Merchandise from all over Europe was pouring into northern Italy, but of even greater significance were exotic goods from the Middle East such as spices, silk clothing, rare hardwood furniture, exquisitely beautiful dyes, and entire libraries of rare books. The flood of products created opportunities for shipbuilders, ship owners, and merchants who began amassing unprecedented fortunes.

Florentines had feared they would be left out of the surging trade industry. Their city, located fifty miles inland from the sea on the Arno River, lacked deepwater harbors to accommodate large oceangoing freighters. Florentine entrepreneurs foresaw the urgency of discovering complementary industries if they expected to grab their fair share of the fortune that was to be made.

The Florentines discovered just what they needed. They were the first to perceive the need for a more efficient financial accounting system than could be achieved using Roman numerals. Florentine entrepreneurs traveling in the Middle East learned of a much faster and more efficient system of counting using Arabic numerals. They learned the system, introduced it to other businessmen in Florence, and within a decade business leaders of most major trading centers in northern Italy were flocking to Florence for accounting expertise.

Establishing Florence as the banking center for all of Europe was the next logi-cal step. As entrepreneurs and companies increased their wealth throughout Europe, they turned their money over to a burgeoning industry of Florentine bankers. The bankers, in turn, pioneered the lending of money at high interest rates allowing businessmen to make money not only at their professions, but also on their surplus funds.

The only problem the bankers faced at the time was the use of many different types of gold, silver, and copper coins minted by many different cities and countries. There were ducats from Venice, livres from Paris, pounds from London, ecus from

A *Florentine bank teller (right) completes a transaction with his customer.*

Use of the florin as international currency originated in Florence.

Bruges, and guilders from Amsterdam. Converting the value of one coin to another had always been problematic until the Florentine bankers established the first standardized currency called the gold florin, the same coin still in use today. By monopolizing the minting of the florin, Florentine bankers now control the money supply of all of Europe. Anywhere travelers go today, the gold florin is the only internationally accepted coin.

As the thirteenth century came to a close, the population of Florence reached sixty thousand and was growing. The city sported grand public buildings built to advertise the city's prosperity over its

rival cities such as Venice, Naples, Siena, and Pisa. At the same time, rival banking families competed with each other to see who could build the most expensive and elaborate villas.

The Discovery of Leisure

Florence was awash in money. The emergence of wealthy families created generations of children who no longer faced the grim reality of tilling the soil behind a plow horse or working at dangerous menial jobs for substandard wages. For the first time in many generations, the children of wealthy Florentine bankers and merchants had ample amounts of leisure time.

Parents quickly filled their children's time with formal education. Learning spread throughout the wealthy families of Florence fueling a discovery of the great Greek and Roman thinkers, artists, and writers whose books had been lost during the chaotic times since the fall of the Roman Empire. This opportunity motivated the wealthy intelligentsia to discover not only what had been lost for centuries, but also to improve and expand upon the discoveries and insights of the ancients.

The spirit of education that supported new ideas and novel answers to basic questions began to spread throughout the neighborhoods of Florence. As innovative thinking blossomed in the arts and sciences, libraries expanded their collections and several Florentine families competed for the fame of claiming the great artists and thinkers of the city as their own.

The combination of wealth and education in the late thirteenth century triggered Florence's fame as the art and literary capital of not only Italy, but of all Europe as well. Dozens of writers, painters, sculptors, and architects began to flourish, working for wealthy Florentines as well as for the Catholic Church. Florence's first great writer, Dante Alighieri, wrote his great work, the *Divine Comedy*, in which he fancifully visits hell, purgatory, and heaven and describes the people residing there. The architect Arnolfo di Cambio began construction on the city's major church, Santa Maria del Fiore; and of the painters, none are more respected for their

The Gold Florin

The use of the florin for travelers as well as for commerce was one of the most revolutionary ideas of its time. When the florin was first instituted in 1252, it was the only gold coin standardized in weight (3.54 grams) and purity (24-carat pure gold). Other coins, both gold and silver, often lacked consistency in weight as well as purity. Adding to the trust that the coin commands throughout Europe is the fact that only Florentine bankers mint the coins. All florins are visually identical bearing the image of John the Baptist, the patron saint of Florence, on one side and the lily, the city's official emblem, on the other. As a result, the florin is the most trusted monetary unit in the European commercial markets and it is the only coin accepted by the papacy.

Travelers are always curious about what the florin will buy. Although prices fluctuate a great deal, a good warhorse will cost 42 florins, a 30-pound steel suit of armor covering the arms and chest, 20 florins. A woman's elegant long dress trimmed in mink may cost as much as one florin as will standard sword and scabbard that is worn on the waist. A year's rent for houses in the better neighborhoods of Florence will cost between 20 and 30 florins; the outskirts of the city, 10 florins; and in the slums, 1 to 2 florins.

If visitors are here to find work, ordinary laborers such as wool and stone workers can expect an annual salary of 40 florins; construction foremen, 80 florins; and a senior government official, 150 florins. When Michelangelo agreed to sculpt the statue *David*, he received 72 florins a year.

Cimabue's Madonna Enthroned *(pictured) and several of his other works can be viewed in Florence.*

Pisa, and the catastrophic Black Plague of 1348 that reduced the city's population from ninety thousand to fifty thousand. Meanwhile the city's inner turmoil incited a series of political struggles among several rival groups competing for control of the city. Most often the wealthy and politically powerful families collided with members of the city's guilds (merchant and artisan unions) such as the bakers, carpenters, and wool and cloth merchants. In spite of this political dissension, the arts continued to flourish in the city creating its international reputation for fine art and architecture.

The House of Medici

The banks of Florence created seemingly unlimited wealth for a handful of families such as the Albizzi, Peruzzi, Bardi, Puci, and Strozzi, but none of these attained the stature of the city's greatest family, the Medici. What made the Medici unique above all others was not their vast fortune—other families had as much and more—but rather their entry into the politics of Florence and their patronage of many of the city's most famous artists.

The fifteenth century dramatically changed Florence. The struggle for control of the city shifted back and forth until the first of the great Medici leaders, Cosimo, emerged as a leading political force in the city. Cosimo was the pope's banker and was thought to be the second wealthiest man in Florence in 1429. Yet, no amount of wealth saved him from

beautiful frescoes than Cimabue and, near the end of the century, Giotto, both of whose works can still be seen throughout the city.

Fourteenth-century Florence was impacted by intermittent wars with neighboring cities such as Lucca, Siena, and

exile by his enemies in 1434. In 1443, Cosimo returned to Florence to the cheers of his followers who kept him in power until his death in 1464.

Cosimo greatly improved the fortunes of Florence from that point forward. His success as a leader was due to his allegiance to the city rather than to his family's fortune or many special interest groups. And in foreign affairs, he sought peace rather than continuing to waste the city's revenue on senseless wars. All citizens respected his views and considered him an honest and fair man. So appreciative were the Florentines for Cosimo's wise leadership that the city council voted to inscribe his tomb with the Latin words *Pater Patria* (Father of the Country).

Cosimo's son Piero took the reigns of power and although his term was shortened by a crippling disease, he continued his father's policies of nurturing the arts, constructing grand new buildings, keeping the peace within the city, and respecting the independence of neighboring cities. Upon his death in 1469, his twenty-year-old son Lorenzo took charge of the family and the city.

Lorenzo was far more loved than his father by the citizens of Florence because he spent more time attending to the welfare of the city and as a patron of the arts than he did to his family's banking business. Referred to by the Florentine as Lorenzo *Il Magnifico* (Lorenzo the Magnificent), his rule was marred by only one attack on the neighboring town of Volterra.

Most of all, Lorenzo was known for his patronage of many of Florence's greatest artists such as Michelangelo, Leonardo da Vinci, and Botticelli, all of whom were regulars at his family's dinner table. Lorenzo died peacefully on April 8, 1492, in his villa in the town of Careggi. Florentines were so moved by his death

Cosimo de' Medici (center) consults with Italian artists and philosophers.

that the entire population attended his funeral.

Lorenzo's son Piero took over leadership of Florence but of all the Medici leaders, he was the most inept. Spoiled, lazy, and contemptuous of commoners, he was incapable of controlling the city. In 1494 he was forced into exile by enemies of the Medici as well as enemies of Florence. Enemies from within the city were led by a monk named Girolamo Savonarola and an audacious writer critical of the Medici,

Niccolò Machiavelli. Enemies from without the city were led by the French king, Charles VIII, whose invasion of northern Italy forced Piero to flee.

Florence Today

Florence is again a peaceful and safe city for visitors. Those who sought to threaten the city have been killed or exiled. Savonarola, after years of criticizing the Medici family and others for living in excessive luxury, and inciting the poor to

The Palazzo Vecchio is well known as the site where the monk Girolamo Savonarola was hanged and then burned at the stake.

oppose them, was finally hanged and his body burned in the Piazza Vecchio before a crowd of thousands. And Machiavelli, the writer who allegedly conspired against the Medici family, is now living in exile in his country estate where he continues to write. As for the French invaders, the Spanish, who hate the French, came to Florence's defense, drove them from the city, and killed their military leader.

Today, in 1512, the Medici have returned from exile. Piero is now dead but his two brothers, Giovanni and Giuliano, have triumphantly returned to rule the city with the blessing of the pope, and hopes are high that the past eighteen years of turbulence are over.

This is the best possible time to visit Florence. The city's leaders are planning several months of festivities celebrating the safe delivery of the city and the return to normalcy under the steady hand of the Medici family. The pope himself is planning a visit and the city is in the process of completing a beautification project that includes erecting new triumphal arches, demolishing several old buildings for splendid new ones, and even erecting a 50-foot-tall obelisk in the *Mercato Nuovo* (New Market). Several festivals are being planned and a new 14-foot-tall marble statue named *David* that was recently carved by Michelangelo Buonarroti, one of the city's many young sculptors, is on public display.

CHAPTER TWO

Weather and Location

The character and tempo of activities in Florence change with the seasons. Winters are somewhat cool and wet compared to southern cities such as Rome and Athens, but travelers from as far north as London and Paris will find the winter weather a welcome relief from their fog, rain, and occasional snow. During the winter months, the average temperature in Florence is 42° F with light rain and drizzle. Generally, winter weather limits most tourist activities to indoor entertainment such as shopping, viewing the city's art treasures, and visits to the great architectural masterpieces that have brought fame to Florence. Although outdoor activities are limited during the winter season, visitors will have more inns and restaurants to choose from and better rates than during the summer season.

Although there is much to be seen and bought inside the art galleries, clothing stores, and jewelry centers, it is not until the Tuscan spring arrives that the city experiences a revival of its energy and beauty. Temperatures warm to a very comfortable 70° F under clear sunny skies as rain dwindles to less than one inch a month. As the temperature improves, all of the outdoor activities come to life and the city's population swells with a tremendous influx of foreign visitors, especially Christian pilgrims passing through on their way to Rome to celebrate Easter.

A second influx of visitors occurs in midsummer when the temperature warms to 85° F and the city becomes an open-air celebration of all of the many cultural attractions that Florence has to offer. It is during the warm summer months that the Florentines and their guests enjoy the city's broad sweeping piazzas—expansive paved squares capable of accommodating thousands of people for a single event. During the spring and summer, citizens and visitors congregate in the large piazzas to enjoy the sights, sounds, and smells of open-air restaurants, food markets, curio shops, sports events, festivals, and general sightseeing.

Tuscany

Florence is the largest and most prosperous of the dozen or so cities that dot the region of Tuscany, an irregular area of about eight thousand square miles in north central Italy. Tuscany is separated from the lush green hills and lakes of the Po Valley to the north by the Apennine Mountains and from the brown dry plains of Rome to the south by low-lying valleys and Lake Trasimeno. Tuscany touches the Ligurian Sea on the west and extends across the Italian peninsula to within a few miles of the Adriatic Sea on the east.

Tuscany is visually a beautiful region but it is also arid. Although rivers flow through the region irrigating wheat and corn crops planted in the valleys, the dry rocky hills provide just enough tough scraggly vegetation and short grasses for sheep and goats to provide wool, meat,

Visitors can enjoy events like the tournament of the Saracens held here in the Piazza della Signoria.

and dairy products. Intermingled with the pastures are other crops that do not rely heavily on rain such as olive and fig trees and vineyards. Local farmers enjoy hunting wild boar, deer, and badger. On rare occasion, the tracks of wolves can be found near remote watering holes.

Florence's place in the arts is also well served by Tuscany's rich veins of gold, silver, and marble used by the hundreds of artisans who have made this city famous throughout Europe. Popular with many visitors is the exquisite gold and silver jewelry made by hundreds of

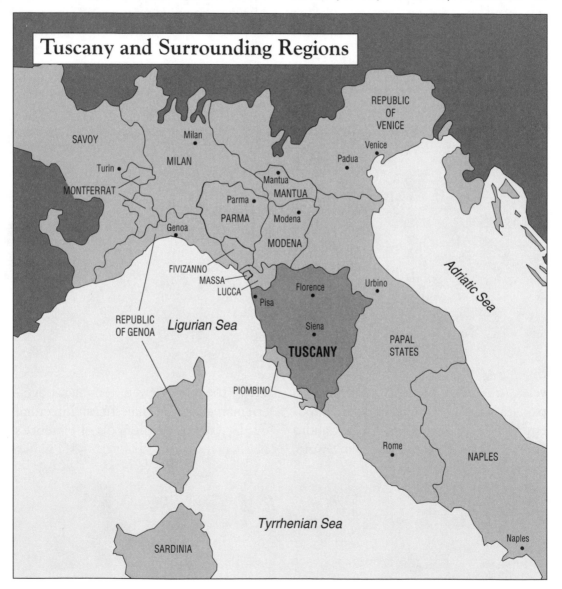

Tuscany and Surrounding Regions

craftsmen in the city. And the marble quarries, especially at the nearby city of Carrara, supply not only the construction trade with building materials but also Florence's most famous sculptors who produce works of art for internationally known entrepreneurs as well as royalty and the popes.

The esthetic beauty of the hills surrounding Florence is another wondrous resource. They have been extolled for the past two hundred years by writers, from Giovanni Boccaccio in the 1300s to modern writers such as Coluccio Salutati. Both men admired the vistas of green valleys punctured by the grayish rocky crags of the Apennine Mountains blending into the blue skies and dusty colors of grape vineyards and olive orchards.

Florentine artists also honor this scenic beauty by including its pastoral settings in the backgrounds of many paintings. Artists speak of the Tuscan light as being clear and sharp, revealing objects without distortions. Some of Florence's most famous paintings were executed in the nearby hills more than two hundred years ago by Florence's most famous painter, Giotto. More recently, the modern painters Leonardo da Vinci, Sandro Botticelli, and the young Raffaello Sanzio, who goes simply by the name Raphael, have also painted the Tuscan landscape into the backgrounds of their works.

Florence

Visitors approaching Florence from any of the main roads will encounter a striking

The beautiful Tuscany countryside shows up in many paintings, including Botticelli's Annunciation.

view of the city long before their arrival. Unlike most walled towns that are perched defensively atop the many hills of Tuscany, Florence is boldly situated in the unprotected valley of the Arno River. First-time visitors approaching the city along the tops of the surrounding hills often stop to rest themselves and water their horses at distant vantage points above the city. Viewed from afar, travelers marvel at the majestic architectural display of the red tile roofs of Florence's many cathedrals, bell towers, and public buildings laid out below them in the valley formed by the winding river.

Florence's location is strategic. Situated in the center of Tuscany, the city occupies a natural transition point for all foot and wagon traffic moving south from the alpine regions of northern Italy and moving north

The Arno River provides Florence with fish, fresh water, and smooth transportation.

from southern Italy. This north-south corridor for travelers, traders, and colliding armies circumvents the rugged Apennine Mountains, which run down the spine of Italy. In addition, since Florence is at the center of this corridor, it is a natural stop along the route for rest and nourishment before moving on.

Of all the major metropolitan cities of Europe, only Florence is located far from the sea or a large river close to the sea. Although the Arno is too small for heavy shipping, it is nonetheless a necessity for Florence. The Florentines recognized long ago that the river could give the city marked commercial advantages over rival

Tuscan hill towns such as Lucca, Livorno, Siena, St. Gimignano, and Volterra, which lack a major water way. In Florence, the Arno turns the mills that grind wheat for breakfast breads and dinner pastas, supplies the fish markets with a variety of fresh catch, and provides traders and travelers with lightweight transportation in the form of flat-bottom boats. It also supplies vast quantities of water for the washing and dying of wool used for the cloth industry, and carries away the city's sewage to the Ligurian Sea.

Florence's location on the Arno and proximity to other Tuscan towns makes it a self-sufficient city. When necessary,

Florentines can subsist exclusively on local resources. Although Florence trades many local goods for items that come from the Middle East and even China, they are not the necessities of life. They are, rather, luxury items for the household and for exotic cooking. In times of economic prosperity, the city is filled with the smells of cinnamon, clove, ginger, and pepper; but when hard times descend upon the city, these savory smells give way to the regional smells of goat, pork, poultry, and fish.

Traveling to Florence

The way to travel to Florence varies according to each traveler's point of departure, pocketbook, and need for protection. Although Florence is a safe city once travelers arrive, getting there can be risky if not carefully planned.

The safest way to travel is by boat. Departing from Genoa, it will take the traveler between three and five days to reach Florence; from Rome, between four and six days; and from Naples, between five and seven days. The best approach is

The Arno River

Florence is a gift of the Arno. Were it not for a turn at this point in the river, Florence would never have become the beautiful city visitors see today. Julius Caesar chose this spot because it offered a safe location for unloading barges.

The Arno begins in dozens of small tributaries near Mount Falterona, east of Florence in the Apennine mountain range. As it moves west, it grows in size until it reaches Florence where, at its widest it is only about one hundred yards across. Even at this width, the river cannot float the large warships and merchant ships seen today entering the coastal ports of Venice, Pisa, Genoa, and Naples.

Flooding, although infrequent, is very much a part of the history of the Arno and of Florence. The winter rains in the Apennines have been known to send torrents of water washing through Florence ripping away all of the bridges, as they did in the famous flood of 1333. During the summers, however, the sun dries up the tributaries to the east reducing the Arno to a few feet of muddy sludge negotiable only by shallow draft barges.

For most Florentines and tourists, the meandering Arno is one of the natural beauties of the city. Small rowboats can be rented to enjoy the view of the city from the river. In the late afternoon, tourists crowd the bridges to watch the sun set as musicians stroll the banks strumming their lutes and playing flutes and recorders.

to board one of the many freighters sailing to Pisa where the Arno empties into the sea. Once at Pisa, take one of the many barges that depart daily for the fifty-mile trip upstream to Florence. If the cost of the barge is too high, the next best approach to Florence is the main dirt road that follows the course of the Arno River. The walk will take two days for young travelers but more for elders. Several small towns along the way provide inns that include breakfast and dinner meals for travelers. A second alternative is to rent a horse at one of the many rental stables in Pisa. The rider will get to Florence in a day and a half, or two days if the horse is pulling a wagon.

For travelers from northern Europe or from cities on the north coast of the Adriatic such as Venice and Ravenna, there are several small rivers that can carry passengers on flat-bottom boats, but some overland travel will be necessary. For travelers who must travel by foot, horse, or wagon, it is recommended that they travel in groups to protect themselves from highwaymen whose profession is stealing from unwary travelers. Recently it has been reported that, south of Florence, unemployed *condottieri* (professional soldiers who sell their services during wars), lie in wait to rob foot travelers and have even killed those who resist.

Robbery raises the issue of how best to protect one's self while traveling. First, it is recommended that travelers avoid clothing that suggests they are

Although horseback is an efficient means of travel, riders must watch out for highway robbers.

Condottieri

Following the dissolution of the Roman Empire, cities throughout western Europe were left defenseless and were overrun by invading armies as well as by neighboring rival towns. To protect themselves, Italian cities without armies hire mercenary soldiers called *condottieri* to defend the towns. For several centuries, the *condottieri* have played a crucial role in the wars within Italy.

The *condottieri* are very often from the ranks of the aristocracy because the cost of providing their own armor and horses is far more than most can afford. Many of these aristocrats organize their own small armies of two or three hundred soldiers called lances, because of the lances they use in battle. One such aristocrat is Federico da Montefeltro, duke of Urbino, who maintains and trains his own army of two hundred lances.

Contracts between a city and an army of mercenaries specify length of service, pay, and such things as how prisoners would be treated and what the lances could and could not steal following a successful battle. Contracts customarily stipulate periods of service between six months and one year. Florence once entered into a contract with Micheletto Attendolo who was paid forty-five thousand florins for providing six hundred lances and four hundred horsemen. Releasing an army at the end of a contract might mean a rival city would hire them and turn them against their former employer.

The largest problem associated with the *condottieri* is unemployment. Without a source of income, many *condottieri* resort to highway robbery that endangers the lives of travelers and merchants hauling merchandise.

wealthy. Second, it is better to carry a small number of gold coins, preferably florins, than a large number of lesser value silver coins. Gold is easily hidden in one's food pack, boots, or other belongings. Another tactic is to convert coins to pearls or gems, which can then be sewn into the lining of clothing. Once in Florence, any number of jewelers will exchange the gems for gold florins.

Although the trip to Florence can sometimes be stressful for travelers, it is well worth the effort. Upon arrival, Florentines welcome all visitors as if they are family and they are eager to make their stay comfortable and memorable. Most of all, Florentines are eager to show off their first-rate accommodations, restaurants, and cultural attractions that make this city the most exciting in all of Europe.

CHAPTER THREE

Arriving in Florence, Where to Stay and Eat

Travelers approaching the city will encounter the five-mile circuit wall completed in 1340 as protection. The wall is especially noticeable from the hills of Chianti to the south of the city and from the hills of Fiesole to the north. This wall, the third in the city's history, is forty feet high. It has seventy-three guard towers that stand sixty feet tall and ten gates that provide passage into and out of the city. Arrival in Florence at least by late afternoon is highly recommended because of the city's curfew.

In order to ensure the safety of citizens and visitors, the *Priori* (city council) imposed a curfew that lasts from sunset to

One of the first things travelers will see upon approaching Florence is the five-mile wall surrounding the city.

Shoemakers are among the tradesmen who greet travelers as they enter Florence in the morning.

sunrise. During this time all ten gates are bolted shut and guarded, and only city guards and a few privileged citizens with special passes are allowed into the city.

Those arriving late must hurry to their inns or homes of family or friends to avoid being found on the streets following the ringing of the evening bells that signal the start of curfew. Anyone found wandering the streets will spend the night in jail and pay a fine. It is common for drunks, who cannot find their way home by evening bells, to sleep in the taverns rather than risk arrest for violating the curfew. If tourists miss the closing of the gates, inns outside the walls can be found to stay in until morning.

At sunrise, morning bells signal the guards to open the ten gates. When the gates are opened, travelers will find a long line of farmers who are the first to enter with their fresh produce for the city. The clattering of their donkey-drawn carts echoing down the narrow cobblestone streets wakes the city. The farmers head straight to the *Mercato Vecchio* (Old Market Place) to sell their goods to the population including owners of restaurants and inns. Joining the farmers early in the morning and adding to the din are workers in the silk and wool trades, the fish and poultry sellers, barbers, construction workers, and a plethora of other merchants.

Travelers entering with the farmers and fishmongers must be a bit wary. Everyone knows that each evening many travelers stranded outside of the walls will be entering the city at sunrise, and as they enter, beggars and pickpockets are likely to

A potter skillfully molds clay in his hands as the wheel spins.

31

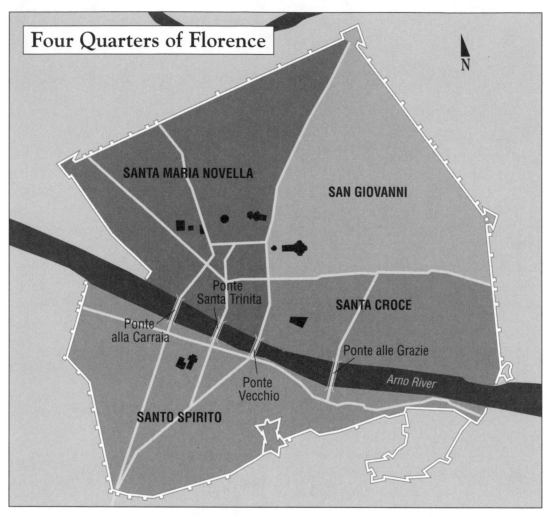

Four Quarters of Florence

SANTA MARIA NOVELLA

SAN GIOVANNI

N

Ponte
Santa Trinita

Ponte
alla Carraia

SANTA CROCE

Ponte alle Grazie

Ponte
Vecchio

Arno River

SANTO SPIRITO

prey on careless visitors. Generally speaking, however, it is safe to walk in the many broad piazzas and narrow streets of Florence because of the presence of uniformed guards.

Getting Around the City

First-time guests to Florence will enjoy exploring the streets of the city. Since the city is flat, few will tire from an active day of meandering. It is not easy to get lost in Florence. Unlike many other flat cities, Florence has three tall landmarks that act as sentinels—the dome of Santa Maria del Fiore, Giotto's bell tower, and the tower of the Palazzo Vecchio—which, when sighted from any point, will guide visitors back to the heart of the city.

To further assist guests, the city is organized into four quarters: Santo Spirito, Santa Croce, Santa Maria Novella, and San Giovanni. Each quarter, in turn, is

Tuscany (see pp. 23–24)

The Duomo (see pp. 56–58)

The Duomo (see p. 57)

Tuscany (see pp. 23–24)

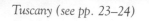

Tuscany (see pp. 23–24)

Tuscany (see p. 23)

Tuscany (see pp. 23–24)

Vineyard (see p. 24)

"Gates of Paradise" (see p. 60)

Tower of the Palazzo Vecchio (see p. 62)

David (*see p. 71*)

Judith and Holofernes (*see p. 68*)

Crucifix *(see p. 66)*

Mona Lisa (*see p. 67*)

The Adoration of the Magi (*see p. 66*)

Trinity (see p. 70)

Madonna of the Goldfinch (*see p. 73*)

Birth of Venus (*see p. 72*)

La Primavera (*see p. 72*)

divided into four districts called *granfaloni* with names such as the Red Lion, the Dragon, the Golden Lion, the Viper, and so on. Each *granfalon* has an identifying color for its banners and traditional dress. Wherever visitors wander, they will know where they are, but if they get confused, locals will be happy to assist them on their way.

Florentines are justifiably proud of the cleanliness of their city, even though pedestrians must be mindful where they step because of the animal traffic, just as in any other city. Nonetheless, unlike most other leading cities of Europe, the major streets in Florence are paved with cobblestone or paving stone and all are either well drained or have sewers to keep them clean. City officials impose fines on those who fail to clean streets in front of their shops and houses or fail to obey orders to dig collection pools to prevent sewage from flowing down streets.

Cleanliness of the City

Florentines are justifiably proud of the cleanliness of their city. Travelers considering a visit to Florence for its architecture, festivals, and artists can add its cleanliness to the list. This is no laughing matter when considering that in 1348, the city was devastated by the Black Plague that killed about forty thousand citizens. Leonardo Bruni, made the following observations about the sanitary conditions in the city in his book, History of the Florentine People:

Every other city is so dirty that the filth created during the night is seen in the early morning by the population and trampled under foot in the streets. Even if there were a thousand palaces in such a city and inexhaustible wealth, even if it possessed an infinite population, still I would always condemn that city as a stinking place and not think highly of it. . . . Hence filthy cities that may in other respects be very good can never be considered to be beautiful. Predictably, of course, Florence is a swan of a different color: Indeed, it seems to me that Florence is so clean and neat that no other city could be cleaner. Surely this city is unique and singular in all the world because you will find here nothing that is disgusting to the eye, offensive to the nose, or filthy under foot. The great diligence of its inhabitants ensures and provides that all filth is removed from the streets, so you see only what brings pleasure and joy to the senses. Moreover, however big a rainstorm, it cannot prevent your walking through the city with dry feet since almost before it falls the rainwater is taken away by appropriately placed gutters. Hence, the cleanliness and dryness that you find only in the rooms of private palaces in other cities, you find in the squares and streets of Florence.

Florence's population of about ninety thousand residents lives within the city's five-mile diameter, nearly all of which is crowded with four- and five-story buildings that function as commercial shops on the street level and apartments on the upper floors. From this rich mix of people and their goods arise odors not found in the countryside. Besides the pungent smells that come forth from the donkeys, dog packs, fish, chickens, freshly slaughtered beef, fresh fruits and vegetables, and sewage and garbage, there is also the smell of those who have not visited the public baths in months.

Where to Stay

The best bet by far when staying in Florence for an extended time is to arrange with family or business associates to stay at their homes. For the visitor who has family or business associates belonging to one of the banking families or the merchant class, accommodations in their homes in the city will be far more pleasant and luxurious than in any of the city's inns.

Public Baths

Public baths, although available, are not widely used in Florence. The wealthy families with homes large enough to accommodate tubs and stoves to heat the water have no need of public baths. The poor bathe in the river or simply with sponges in their homes. Unlike the ancient Romans for whom attending public baths was a social outlet, Florentines typically do not like bathing any more often than necessary, one or twice a month.

Although public baths are available within the city, they are small and simple. Most provide a small private room and a basin of water, cold for those on a small budget, warm but not hot for those willing to spend more money. The price of the bath includes the use of a bar of soap, which must be left in the room for the next customer. The better soaps are made from olive oil and the lower quality ones from animal fats. Tallow, the fat from cattle, is the chief fat used. Some public baths offer massages, which many citizens believe are sinful and should be outlawed.

When the Black Plague swept through Florence in 1348, the public baths were closed because the authorities of the time thought these baths promoted the spread of the plague. Without bathing, the population increased their use of heavy scents placed in wax and spread over the skin and hair.

Parents visiting the city with adolescent children might want to keep their children out of the public baths. Some of the baths attract an unsavory crowd without much else to do but spread idle gossip.

Most banking families have branch offices in other major cities in Italy and anticipate that business travelers will stay with them when visiting Florence. If business associates arrive in the summer, they will probably be invited to the family's villa in the quiet Tuscan hills nearby. While passing the summer in his villa outside the city's walls, Cardinal Pietro Bembo wrote, "I hear no noise but that of some nightingales vying with each other around me. . . . I read and write as much as I want; I ride, walk, and often go for strolls in the wood I have at the bottom of the garden."[1]

For those without family or business accommodations, all four quarters of the city have many inns for travelers. The prices for rooms are determined by their amenities. The most economical rooms are usually located on the first floor of inns on the outskirts of the city where the noise and smells of the street are most noticeable. These accommodations will have small windows or none at all, and they are unheated in the winter. Inside the room, patrons will find a bed and one mattress, usually stuffed with hay and set on ropes that must be tightened each night to prevent the mattress from sagging down to the floor. Renters should not expect to find a table or chair. Sometimes tourists on tight budgets will share a room. Innkeepers commonly allow a family or group of four strangers to share the cost of a room for the night.

For wealthier travelers, the best inns are near the center of the city where the rooms are large, have windows for fresh air, and are heated in the winter. Heaters are either fireplaces for travelers who can afford them, or *scaldini* (warming pans filled with hot charcoal). Beds for the affluent travelers will have two mattresses stuffed with goose down, a table and chair, and candles for night use. Walls will be whitewashed and clean but not painted. There may be a sink for washing before going to sleep and access to a latrine that empties down a tile drain spout to the sewer below. For an additional small sum, the air in the room can be sweetened with burning herbs or with scented wax hanging from the ceiling. During the summer, upper-story windows are shaded by an awning attached to the exterior of the building.

Some inns provide meals for customers willing to pay higher rates. Two meals a day are available, one at about ten in the morning and the other at seven or eight in the evening depending upon the season. The meals served at inns are generally quite simple because of sumptuary laws passed by the *Priori* that forbid the sale of foods considered extravagant. If any meals are served, they consist of bread, vegetable soups, beans, cabbages, and potatoes. Cheese and eggs are readily available as are polenta and pasta made from flour and eggs. In addition to the problem of the sumptuary laws, few inns have adequate kitchen facilities. Consequently, many travelers are forced to eat their meals uncooked wherever they buy their food, or if they have extra money they can find many restaurants in the city, some of which dismiss the sumptuary laws.

Trattorias like this one provide warm, hearty food for tourists who need meals to go.

Eating on the Go

Many travelers prefer to eat on the run. Some prefer this approach to save time and money while others wish to experience the color and flavors of each *granfalon*'s neighborhood open-air market.

The food at the many open-air markets, often called farmers' markets, is always fresh but uncooked. Nonetheless, breads, cheeses, and fruits can be purchased in small quantities for a single meal to be eaten on the spot along with smoked and salted meats sold by the slice. Wines and fruit juices are available to be drunk directly from the barrel for a small price per mouthful.

As an alternative to eating at the open-air markets and the sit-down restaurants, famished tourists can grab a quick bite at a trattoria (inexpensive sidewalk café) that serves a few simple inexpensive meals, some of which are warmed.

Favorites are *ribollita,* served lukewarm and made with Tuscan bread, vegetables, and beans; *peposo,* a beef stew made with Chianti wine, black peppercorns, and butternut squash; and a local Tuscan salad called *panzanella* made with bread, cucumbers, and tomatoes.

For those seeking heartier fare, the city has a rich selection of restaurants that will suit anyone's budget.

Finding a Good Restaurant

Restaurants complying with the sumptuary laws are popular with travelers of modest means because although the food is basic, the portions are large. Besides the usual selection of peasant breads, these inns serve simple foods such as lasagna or pasta in *savour sango* (red meat sauce with wine and raisins) and some restaurants serve *fegatelli* (liver sausage with spinach or carrots). Goats' milk cheese and the dessert *pinocchiato* (pine nut pudding) can be found on special occasions.

For travelers willing to spend more money, a greater variety of foods that are seasoned with expensive spices imported from the Middle East is available, but that will increase the price of a meal by as much as 100 percent. Several restaurants serve Florentine specials such as fish pies and chicken soup spiced with ginger, nutmeg, and cloves; chicken parts seasoned with bay leaves, saffron, and parsley; duck and rabbit sprinkled with grated cheese, and occasionally, roasted meats smothered

Rules of Etiquette

Eating in public has become so common that Giovanni della Casa has written a book called the Galateo, *describing proper manners when eating with others either in the piazzas or in one of the city's many taverns. The following are some of the more important rules to observe in order to avoid offending others:*

- Do not chew noisily like the French.
- Do not crouch over your food.
- Do not hiccup.
- Avoid rubbing your teeth with your napkin or, worse still, with your fingers.
- Do not scratch yourself, or spit.
- Do not offer your neighbor a pear or other fruit from which you have already bitten.
- After blowing your nose, do not look into your handkerchief as if pearls or rubies had been deposited in it.
- Do not put a leg on the table.
- Avoid spitting into your fingers.

in honey. For those with hearty appetites on Sundays, restaurant owners will roast large portions of beef, goat, and chunks of pork. Indeed, Florentines and their guests eat well. According to the contemporary Florentine writer Giovanni Villani, "as many as 30,000 pigs are brought into the city each year, together with 70,000 sheep, 20,000 goats, and 4,000 oxen and calves."[2]

Meals on special occasions, such as the celebration of religious festivals, are even more varied. Although they obvi-

The Spice Trade

Two hundred years ago, the diet of all Florentines as well as all other Europeans was bland at best and often unhealthy. Because of the lack of preservation methods and poor quality, meats required spices to make them edible. When the crusaders returned to Europe from the Middle East, they brought with them an assortment of spices never before seen by Europeans.

The popularity of spices soon went far beyond flavoring foods. Pepper, for example, is used extensively in cooking but is also used for a tonic, a stimulant, an insect repellent, and an aphrodisiac. Spices are so rare and sought after that they also are a form of currency in remote villages. Spices can also be used to pay fines and mortgages, to buy land, to buy arms, or to pay taxes. In addition to using spices for flavoring food and as currency, they also are used to preserve meat and fish for long periods of time.

The Italian merchants who sponsored these trade caravans became very wealthy and influential. The cost and risk is high but the rewards are great. It is said that a merchant can ship six boats loaded with spices, lose five, and still make a profit when he sells the sixth.

Merchants from the East transport spices and other goods to Italy.

The most popular spices found in Florence today include cinnamon from China and Burma; nutmeg from the Banda Islands; cloves from only two islands, Ternate and Tidore (south of Indonesia), which are also known as the Spice Islands; and pepper that is grown only in India, although there are some poor substitutes found in other places.

Sit-down restaurants provide a variety of tasty food and large portions.

ously violate the sumptuary laws, no one is fined because of the religious holidays. Exotic foods such as veal, dove, and trout are brought into the city. Melons from warm Middle East countries are enjoyed as desserts alongside *berlingozzi* (sweet cakes made of sugar, eggs, cheese, and fruit). For those wishing the most sumptuous desserts possible, sculptured marzipan sprinkled with spiced cherries can be bought for a hefty price.

For those travelers and citizens of Florence with limitless bank accounts, the fare offered at the city's most expensive restaurants becomes increasingly extravagant as the enforcement of the sumptuary laws becomes increasingly unlikely. Dishes such as capons in white sauce with pomegranate seeds, minced goat livers seasoned with ginger, peacock, pheasant, whole roasted pig, eels from the local rivers, and sturgeon from as far away as Russia can be found.

In keeping with the exotic foods, the decorations at these expensive food houses rival the food itself. Each table is set with as many layers of tablecloths as there are courses, and as each course is finished, one tablecloth is removed and the entire complement of glassware and silverware is replaced.

Once visitors have found good lodging and places to eat, it is time to investigate the city. The best way to start is with the city's famous architecture. Fortunately, the major architectural works are all compactly located in the heart of the city making it possible to visit all of them in a single day.

Architectural Monuments of Florence

Many of Florence's greatest treasures are architectural monuments. In the heart of the city, occupying the two adjoining piazzas, del Duomo and San Giovanni, visitors will find the three most impressive examples of Florentine monumental architecture: the cathedral Santa Maria del Fiore, Giotto's bell tower, and the Baptistery. These three white and green marble structures stand within twenty-five feet of each other and for travelers here for only a day's visit, they are the city's most popular and most impressive attractions.

Santa Maria del Fiore

Santa Maria del Fiore—Saint Mary of the Flowers—is most commonly referred to as the Duomo, meaning House of God. It is the architectural gem of the city as well as the largest and most elegant cathedral in Europe. Standing 370 feet above the streets below, with a red tile dome 140 feet in diameter, the green and white marble cathedral is a most distinctive landmark, visible for miles along the approach to the city.

Located in the cultural center of the city, the cathedral will overwhelm visitors with its size and height. Spectators standing a few feet away from the cathedral while looking straight up will experience the sense that the dome is falling on them. Visitors willing to climb the 467 stone steps to the top of the cupola will enjoy an unobstructed view of the city as well as a panoramic view of the beautiful Tuscan landscape.

Begun in 1296 by the Florentine Arnolfo di Cambio, the cathedral was completed in 1436 by the Florentine architect Filippo Brunelleschi. Construction of the foundation and walls was completed in 1336, but the structure sat domeless in the rain and sun for the next one hundred years because no architect or engineer at that time knew how to build a dome large enough to span the octagonal walls of the apse, the area of the altar. The man who would eventually conceive the mathematics needed to support such a tremendous size and weight as well as the mechanics to put it in place, Filippo Brunelleschi, had not yet been born.

In 1418, the arts council of Florence announced a competition for the design and construction of the dome. Brunelleschi stepped forth with a wood model of an elliptical dome—shaped like half an egg—reinforced with eight cross-braced ribs that would be exposed on the exterior of a red tiled dome.

To provide sufficient light in the interior during the day, Brunelleschi placed eight large round windows in the walls supporting the dome and a stone lantern of eight long windows on the very top of the dome. The lantern added seventy feet to the total height of the cathedral. All who have seen this dome agree that with its long vertical lines and terracotta red tiles, it is the most beauti-ful dome in the world. The contemporary Florentine writer, Alberti, asked the rhetorical question,

Who is so dull or jealous that he would not admire Filippo the architect in face of this gigantic building, rising above the vaults of heaven? It is wide enough to receive in its shade all the people of Tuscany, and built without the aid of any truss work or mass of timber. [3]

Brunelleschi's dome, completed in 1436

Giotto's Tower, completed in 1359

Santa Maria del Fiore and Giotto's Tower

57

Most visitors do not take the time to enter the cathedral but the interior is just as dramatic as the dome. Visitors are struck by the enormity of the interior, 497 feet long and 123 feet wide. The altar sits directly below the dome where visitors can experience the breathtaking view, straight up.

After exiting the Duomo, a quick left turn will lead to the third tallest structure in Florence, the city's most revered bell tower, Giotto's tower.

Giotto's Tower

Giotto's tower is the 278-foot-tall bell tower designed and begun in 1334 by the painter Giotto, but not completed until 1359 by the builder Francesco Talenti.

This elegant multicolored marble bell tower with a 49-foot-square base is considered by most travelers to be the most beautiful bell tower in all of Italy. They even say that it is more beautiful than the bell tower in Pisa, which is severely leaning and some fear may topple over.

The tower is covered with the same colors of marble as Santa Maria del Fiore to give the two buildings the appearance of being a matched set. The lower story of the tower is decorated with a band of sculpted scenes carved by Andrea Pisano. The three upper stories of the tower also have sculptures and enormous vertical windows that flood the interior stairs with light.

The tower offers opportunity for a visitor to climb up its 414 stairs for a close-

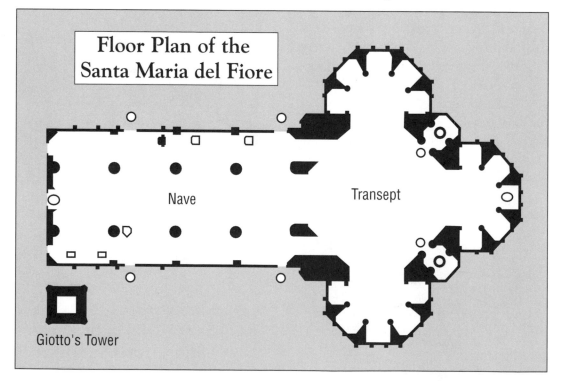

Floor Plan of the Santa Maria del Fiore

Nave

Transept

Giotto's Tower

The Baptistery

Ghiberti's bronze doors

up view of the dome of the Duomo as well as a stunning view of the surrounding Tuscan countryside. When exiting the tower, head directly across the piazza to the third and oldest example of monumental architecture in Florence, the Baptistery.

The Baptistery

This building, which today is dedicated to St. John the Baptist, is considered the oldest church in the city although its origins are uncertain. Before it was dedicated to St. John, it was the city's primary cathedral. The unusual octagonal shape of the building suggests a seventh-century origin although none of the original building remains. The exterior diameter is identical to the diameter of the dome of the Duomo, 140 feet. City historians estimate that around 1150, the original sandstone walls were covered with the white Carrara and green Prato marble inlay that visitors see today.

Entry to the Baptistery is through three pairs of bronze doors that are now more widely admired than the building itself. In 1401, the city's art commission announced a competition to design the east pair. Seven of the finest artists in Tuscany took part in the competition, among them Filippo Brunelleschi and the sculptor and goldsmith Lorenzo Ghiberti, who was only twenty-three at the time. Each artist submitted a sample work, and the commission judged those of Brunelleschi and Ghiberti the best and offered each the job of executing one door of the pair. Brunelleschi, however, insulted by the suggestion that Ghiberti was his equal, left Florence for Rome and the job of creating both doors to his rival.

Ghiberti began work on the two doors in 1403 and finally in 1424 hung the twenty-eight panels depicting biblical scenes. The commission acclaimed the doors as more beautiful than they had anticipated and contracted with Ghiberti in 1425 to sculpt a second pair for the north entrance. Completed in 1452, this second pair of doors, each decorated with five large panels depicting scenes from the Old Testament, is even more beautiful than the first. When the doors were first revealed to the public, the painter and sculptor Michelangelo named them the "Gates of Paradise" because he believed they were worthy of gracing paradise.

It has long been of interest to many Florentines that the interior of the Baptistery repeats the outside octagonal configuration. Once inside, the visitors' eyes are drawn to the eight segments of the ceiling, each of which contains a mosaic depicting a biblical scene. To this day, these mosaics remain the most beautiful in the city. After the ceiling, the eight walls dominate the view, each decorated differently with many colors of marble panels. The floor is covered with marble giving it the appearance of a carpet, and dates back four hundred years to the twelfth century. Since this building was built for baptisms, its central basin is used for that purpose each New Year's Eve, when all children born the previous year are baptized.

If time is still available, a short four- or five-block walk from the Baptistery toward the river will lead to one of the city's oldest and most famously decorated churches, Orsanmichele.

Orsanmichele

Orsanmichele is a strange church. Located in the heart of Florence, its brown stone blocks and rectangular two-story design make it look more like a warehouse than a church. That is because, although Orsanmichele started as a church, it was later converted into a grain market, then back to a church, and finally back to a grain warehouse. Originally called San Michele in Orto (St. Michael's in the Garden), the name was later simplified to Orsanmichele.

The original church was significantly altered by the Florentine architect Arnolfo di Cambio around 1290 when the people of Florence recognized the need for a centrally located market and warehouse to sell and distribute the many types of grains brought into the city each

"The Gates of Paradise"

More tourists visit the Baptistery to see the "Gates of Paradise" than enter the building. Ghiberti's second set of doors for the Baptistery is considered by all Florentines to be his greatest work. Standing sixteen and a half feet tall with a width of nine and a half feet, these thirty-four-thousand-pound bronze doors are visited by thousands of visitors each year. Ghiberti and his assistants spent twenty-seven years (1425–1452) completing these doors for which he was paid twenty-two-thousand florins, the most ever paid for a major work of art.

Ghiberti divided the twin doors into five panels per door set in a vertical column. Each of the ten panels is roughly two and a half feet square. Each panel depicts a well-known scene described in the Old Testament, such as the Creation of Adam, the Sacrifice of Abel, the Drunkenness of Noah, and Moses Receiving the Ten Commandments. The ten panels are bordered by a continuous sequence of small heads, floral motifs, and niches that contain small statues of Old Testament prophets.

The praise that the doors have received is due to their accuracy, rich detail, and depth of relief. Ghiberti was especially adept at this type of detail because of his initial training as a goldsmith and then a sculptor. Visitors gazing at the panels are able to see the details of facial wrinkles, muscles and joints in legs and arms, as well as the expressions of eyes that convey the feeling of each character. The depth of the panels, as much as two inches, creates a three-dimensional character much more pronounced than has ever been seen before.

Ghiberti set a new standard of excellence that forced all sculptors following him to perfect their craft, elevating the quality of the work of all Florentine sculptors.

day. The grain bins were located on the upper floors and chutes to the street below were added for loading the grain sacks onto carts.

Entering the church, the visitor will be able to see how the warehouse operated. Looking upward, one can see the opening in the ceiling through which the grain and oats brought here for storage were hoisted up with winches and pulleys. When the warehouse was altered again and converted into a church between 1367–1380, the interior rectangular hall was divided into two naves, one of them containing a magnificent marble tabernacle with a statue of the *Death of the Virgin* sculpted by Andrea di Orcagna at the rear.

When exiting, visitors can admire the statues that surround the exterior of the church in what is considered the most impressive outdoor sculpture gallery in the city. The exterior walls have fourteen deep niches, each containing a larger-than-life-sized statue of a patron saint of one of the city's major guilds such as the wool merchants, blacksmiths, silk merchants, butchers, and goldsmiths. The series ends with the armor makers' statue of St. George holding a shield and spear.

A two-block walk toward the river will take guests to another of Florence's unorthodox examples of large-scale architecture, the *Palazzo Vecchio*, located in the Piazza della Signoria.

The Palazzo Vecchio

The Palazzo Vecchio (Old Palace) has the looks of a cube-shaped fortress. It is one of the masterpieces of fourteenth-century architecture. Constructed between 1299 and 1314 by the architect Arnolfo di Cambio the sixty-foot-tall exterior stone walls, quarried from the nearby hill of Boboli, give the palace a rough and sturdy look. Despite its military appearance and availability for use in case of war, the palace was built to function as the place of business for the *Priori*.

At the top of the palace is di Cambio's daring solution to the problem of creating both a civic building and a fortress—a wide projecting crenellated gallery supported by small arches and the nine coats of arms of the city painted in repetition below the arches. The crenellations, or notches in the tops of the walls, are used for defense of the palace. Defenders, high above the attackers, step into the notches to shoot arrows, then quickly duck behind the wall for protection while drawing their next arrow. The crenellations are also used for dropping stones or boiling oil on the attacking forces.

To cap off the palace, di Cambio added a 309-foot tower (see p. 40). Of all the towers in Florence, this one, named after the architect, is the tallest. The tower is a curiosity to visitors of Florence, not because of its height or shape, but rather because it soars up unexpectedly from one wall, not in the middle of the palace. As a

Visitors will surely notice the off-center tower of the Palazzo Vecchio and marvel at its height.

result of its position, off center along one wall, viewers frequently comment that it appears the entire palace might topple over.

The reason di Cambio located the tower on the one wall that borders the Piazza della Signoria is partly to comply with the lack of symmetry of the piazza, and partly to provide those willing to climb to the top an arresting view of the activities and people in the city's most frequented piazza below.

The main entry is beneath the tower, and as visitors pass through it from the Piazza della Signoria, they emerge into a beautiful courtyard. A fountain at the center sports a cupid and dolphin sculpture by Andrea del Verrocchio. From this courtyard, ramps on the right and the left provide access to the upper levels where the view to the piazza is worth the hike. For art lovers, on the first floor is a large room called *Salone dei Cinquecento* designed by Antonio da Sangallo and Francesco di Domenico and frescoed by Michelangelo and Leonardo da Vinci.

CHAPTER FIVE

Finding the Masters

Florence is alive with art shops where artisans and their young *garzoni* (apprentices) work on paintings, sculptures, and decorative jewelry. Florentine society still views art primarily as a craft, not a respected profession, even though a growing number of artists are becoming recognized for their genius.

The leading tourist attraction of Florence is its world-renowned collection of sculpture, paintings, and frescoes. Although the architectural masterpieces of the city are easy to locate, for those who enjoy strolling the narrow streets of Florence, finding the paintings, frescoes, and sculptures requires more diligence. In spite of the fact that the city has a clear need for a museum to house its many masterpieces, such an undertaking remains a long way off. In the meantime, visitors will need to visit the many churches, piazzas, and palaces that house the city's priceless art collection.

Fortunately for visitors, most of the art in the city has been purchased by either the church or one of the city's prominent banking families, especially the Medici, for public display. The following guide will take art enthusiasts to the best works of many of the city's most renowned artists.

Giotto

One of the hill towns just outside of Florence in the Mugello Valley is the birthplace of Giotto. Born from peasant stock around 1276, Giotto di Bondone grew up knowing little more than how to care for goats and sheep, although many accounts claim that at an early age he demonstrated an eager artistic mind.

One day while tending his sheep, the youthful Giotto was sketching nature scenes in the dirt when the most famous painter of the time, Cimabue, a nickname meaning "ox head," was passing through the Mugello Valley. Coming upon the young boy and seeing his sketches, Cimabue invited Giotto to study art with him in Florence.

As Giotto's fame grew, leading artists recognized that he was pushing beyond the old tired gloomy art of the previous centuries to create an entirely new style. His paintings not only depicted human happiness but also the illusion of three-dimensional depth through his innovative use of perspective. Vasari, an Italian painter, made this observation about Giotto:

In my opinion, painters owe to Giotto, the Florentine painter, exactly the same debt they owe to nature . . . . It was, indeed, a great miracle that in so gross and incomplete an age, Giotto could be inspired to such good purpose that by his work he completely restored the art of design, of which his contemporaries knew little or nothing.[4]

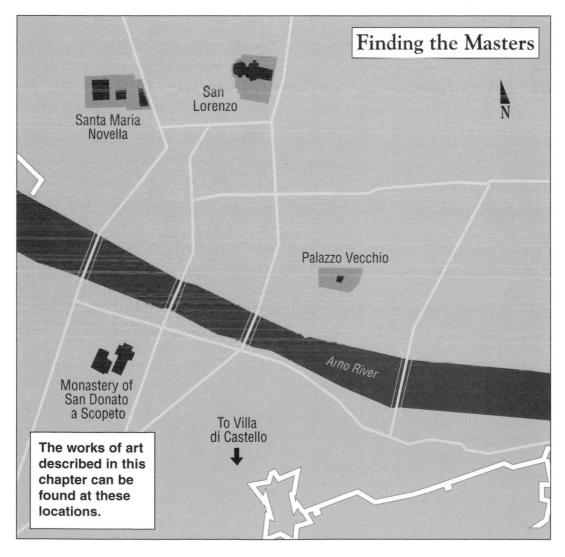

Finding the Masters

Santa Maria Novella

San Lorenzo

N

Palazzo Vecchio

Arno River

Monastery of San Donato a Scopeto

To Villa di Castello

The works of art described in this chapter can be found at these locations.

Giotto painted the Crucifix, *which now hangs in the convent of Santa Maria Novella.*

Giotto's *Crucifix*

Visitors to Florence are fortunate to be able to go to the Dominican convent of Santa Maria Novella to view the *Crucifix* (see p. 43) that Giotto painted between 1288 and 1290 when he was still a young boy. His genius is apparent in this painting of Christ on the cross. Visitors will see that it is more realistic than earlier renderings because of its accurate representation of the human body and the illusion that the foreground of the painting appears to be closer to the viewer than the background, which looks very far away.

Directions: Santa Maria Novella is located two blocks from the Arno on line with the Ponte alla Carraia or about four hundred yards due west from the Duomo.

Leonardo da Vinci

Leonardo was born in 1452 in the small town of Vinci, not far from Florence. About 1466, he worked as a *garzone* to Andrea del Verrocchio, the leading Florentine painter and sculptor of his day. Many visitors are surprised to learn that da Vinci executed a very small number of paintings and that most of the ones in Florence remain unfinished. Although da Vinci now lives in Milan working for Ludovico Sforza, duke of Milan, many here hope he will return one day.

The Adoration of the Magi

A trip to the Monastery of San Donato a Scopeto is well worth the time to see da Vinci's first large painting, *The Adoration of the Magi* (see p. 45), although it remains unfinished. He worked on it in 1481 and 1482, and now that he is sixty years old and in failing health, senior monastery officials are frustrated by his refusal to return and finish the task he began more than thirty years ago.

The Adoration of the Magi, which da Vinci painted on wood slats, is considered by art lovers to be one of the most revolutionary works in the city. The painting depicts the three wise men—the magi—surrounding Mary who is holding the baby Jesus on her lap. Da Vinci learned from earlier masters the art of geometrically laying out his composition in the form of a triangle. At the center of this work are four figures rendered in very light color, forming a triangle with Mary and Jesus at the apex and two of the magi to her left and right in the foreground. Gesturing hands, a hallmark of da Vinci's style, all point toward Mary and Jesus except for one pointing heavenward to indicate the presence of God.

Artists consider this a masterpiece because da Vinci artfully displays two new painting techniques: chiaroscuro, the interplay of light and dark tones; and sfumato, defining forms by blending instead of outlining. Although the work is still incomplete, his application of chiaroscuro is artfully illustrated in the group of admirers to the right in this painting. The masterful use of light tones, deftly applied as little more than isolated lines and swirls in the depth of dark tones, give only vague outlines to the many people in this crowd. They appear to be a boiling mass mystically swirling out of the darkness, drawn to the light tones of Mary and Jesus. True to the intent of chiaroscuro, we see a general surge of shadowy figures without seeing the individuality of each one.

The background of this work displays the use of sfumato. The distant trees, moun-

tains, and horses blend, like smoke, into a hazy dreamlike setting that the viewer might associate with idealistic biblical settings such as the Garden of Eden where all creatures exist in perfect harmony.

Many artists in the city talk about a painting of da Vinci's that he calls *La Gioconda*. Others call it the *Mona Lisa* (see p. 44). One remarkable feature of this portrait of a woman is that da Vinci actually completed the work. Artists who have

Leonardo da Vinci is known for using geometry to place the compositions of his paintings.

viewed it regard it as one of the greatest paintings they have seen. If visitors to Florence would like to see this completed work by the great master, they will need to locate da Vinci for a viewing because he keeps it with him at all times and refuses to display it publicly.

Directions: The Monastery of San Donato a Scopeto is across the river in the district of Santo Spirito. Cross the Ponte Vecchio, then turn right on the first street. The monastery will be one block on the left, overlooking the river.

Donatello

Born within the city walls of Florence in 1387, Donato di Bardi grew up with the name Donatello, meaning Little Donato. Donatello's early apprenticeship was as a goldsmith, not a sculptor, and it probably began in the workshop of the great architect Brunelleschi in 1399 when Donatello was twelve. At the age of seventeen, Donatello received the opportunity to work as an apprentice at the shop of the most famous sculptor of the time, Lorenzo Ghiberti, who was in the process of designing and executing his bronze doors for the Baptistery in Florence. The best place in the city to see several pieces of Donatello's work is at the Orsanmichele church but his largest and most dramatic statue, *Judith and Holofernes*, is in the Palazzo della Signoria.

Judith and Holofernes

Although this sculpture (see p. 42) was commissioned by Cosimo de Medici as a centerpiece for a fountain in the garden of his private palace, it now stands in the Palazzo della Signoria. One of his last works, Donatello executed this seven-foot-nine-inch bronze statue between 1455 and 1460.

The genius of Donatello is illustrated in two areas of this sculpture. First, he was the only sculptor of the time to portray faces with detailed expressions that

Donatello (pictured) trained as an apprentice to Lorenzo Ghiberti, designer of the bronze doors of the Baptistery.

communicate the person's inner feelings. Second, Donatello was the only sculptor who portrayed his characters as if they were in motion. He accomplished this feat by twisting their bodies at the hip, shifting their weight to one foot, and positioning the arms as if they were moving.

This is Donatello's most electrifying of all of his works, depicting a story from the Old Testament. This masterpiece portrays a woman, Judith, at the moment before the sword she swings strikes the neck of the kneeling Assyrian general Holofernes. The extraordinary power of this piece is evident to the viewer looking up at the act of decapitation frozen an instant before the fatal blow. Judith stands over Holofernes pulling his head upward by his hair while standing on his wrist, pinning him to the ground so he cannot escape his inevitable fate. Holofernes, juxtaposed to Judith, looks dazed, entirely incapable of comprehending the finality of the moment.

Directions: The Palazzo Vecchio is located just two blocks north of the Arno between the Ponte Vecchio and the Ponte alle Grazie or about a quarter of a mile south of the Duomo.

Masaccio

Masaccio was born in the small Tuscan village of San Giovanni Valdarno in 1401 and is considered by modern painters to be the first great modern painter after Giotto. While Masaccio's brilliant use of perspective came from his studies of Giotto, his depiction of natural light is his own hallmark, and most modern painters owe a debt to him for developing it. Masaccio

Masaccio is known for his ability to express natural light in his paintings.

died at the early age of twenty-seven, so he had only enough time to complete four masterpieces. One of his finest in Florence is the *Trinity* that he painted in 1424, and it is well worth visiting the church of Santa Maria Novella to see it. So well known was Masaccio's talents as a painter that da Vinci said of him:

Masaccio was an excellent imitator of nature, universally acclaimed, an able composer, pure and unadorned: because he dedicated himself only to the representation of what is true: and to the perspective of his figures: he was certainly of greater skill and foresight than others of those times: and most able, being so young as to die at the age of twenty-seven.[5]

The *Trinity*

This large fresco (see p. 46), 21¹/₂ feet tall by 10 feet wide, overwhelms visitors standing before it. The secret to viewing this great fresco, however, is to move to the back of the church from where it was intended to be seen. From the back, viewers will see the whole composition, which is of Jesus on the cross flanked by Mary and St. John just below him.

All the figures are inside of an arch and as viewers look at the work, they will recognize that the background scenery looks very far away while the main figures look very close. This illusion is the earliest excellent example of the use of perspective that Masaccio learned from Giotto and then perfected—the ability to depict depth or distance on a flat surface.

Equally revolutionary is Masaccio's mastery of scale. In this large fresco, all elements, the arch, the two columns, the cross, and the people are painted in correct proportion to each other. In addition, the anatomy of Christ on the cross is also in correct proportion to the human body. This careful attention to scale improved upon Giotto.

As impressive as the perspective are the remarkably beautiful colors Masaccio created and applied to the wall in the church. Brilliant reds and deep blues for clothing are in stark contrast to the subtle flesh tones of Christ and the honey color of the painted marble columns.

Directions: Santa Maria Novella is located just two long blocks from the Arno on line with the Ponte alla Carraia or about four hundred yards due west from the Duomo.

Michelangelo sculpted David, *the most popular attraction in all of Florence.*

Michelangelo

Born in 1475 in a nearby village, Michelangelo's family moved to Florence when he was small. By the time he was thirteen, his keen artistic sense gained him entrance to the house of the Medici where he studied sculpture and painting. Following a two-year stay in Rome where he sculpted the *Pieta* for the pope, Michelangelo returned to Florence in 1500 with a reputation as the best sculptor in Italy and was awarded a huge block of Carrara marble to sculpt by Florence's art commission.

The hallmark of Michelangelo's works that places him at the pinnacle of the pantheon of contemporary artists is his quest for perfection. Michelangelo strives for the highest quality possible in his rendering of the torso and in expressing the spirit of his subjects in their faces.

Nowhere in Florence can visitors better see the power of his work than at the piazza in front of the Palazzo Vecchio where his *David* now stands. Regarded by other Florentine artists as well as casual visitors to Florence as the best sculpture in all of Italy, this piece attracts more visitors than any other single work in Florence.

David

Michelangelo's best-known creation, *David* (see p. 41), was executed a few years ago between 1501 and 1504. The 14-foot-tall white marble statue shows an alert David of the Old Testament waiting for his adversary, Goliath.

Michelangelo portrayed his *David* as a powerful young man (unlike his predecessors who portrayed David in the biblical tradition of a small timid youth). With this huge block of marble at his disposal, Michelangelo broke from biblical as well as artistic tradition by depicting David as more than two times larger than life size in a pose emphasizing superb physical strength and a fixed stare of intractable defiance.

Michelangelo had studied Greek sculpture and learned that the importance of the person's spirit was of equal importance to the body. The spirit of David, can be plainly seen, both in his body and his facial expression. Standing with his sling over his shoulder, *David*'s calm stance and riveting stare epitomize the confidence and courage of a victorious warrior. The placement of the weight of *David*'s body on the left leg conveys a casual confidence in his ability to spring to action at a moment's notice.

Michelangelo completed the statue inside of a shed and when it was time to unveil it in 1512 to the citizens of Florence, Luca Landucci says, "It took four days to reach the piazza. It was moved along by more than forty men."[6] All Florentines hope that many more of his works will beautify the city in the future.

Directions: The Palazzo Vecchio is located just two blocks north of the Arno between the Ponte Vecchio and the Ponte alle Grazie or about a quarter of a mile south of the Duomo.

Botticelli

Sandro Botticelli was born in Florence in 1445 as Alessandro di Mariano Filipepi but

Botticelli was employed by the Medici and painted both La Primavera *and* Birth of Venus.

quickly acquired the nickname Botticelli, meaning "little barrel." As is the case with many famous artists, Botticelli began as a goldsmith and later moved on as a *garzone* to the painter Fra Filippo Lippi. By 1470, Botticelli had his own workshop and was employed by the Medici as a portrait artist for their family.

Botticelli's fame is derived from two revolutionary innovations he brought to painting. First, he is one of the earliest painters to render scenes that combine both pagan and Christian religious themes, and second, he pioneered the rendering of slender elegant figures that appear to be blown by the wind while bathed in soft golden light.

Raphael (pictured) adapted the techniques of Michelangelo and da Vinci in his own paintings.

La Primavera and Birth of Venus

These two paintings by Botticelli, considered his most famous, can be viewed at the Villa di Castello. Both were commissioned by Lorenzo di Pierfrancesco de' Medici, cousin of the more-well-known Lorenzo de' Medici. *La Primavera* (*Spring*) (see p. 48 bottom) was painted during 1477 and 1478 while the *Birth of Venus* (see p. 48 top) was painted in 1483. Both of these major works are well worth the journey to the villa.

Looking at the 10-by-6 ½-foot *Primavera*, one sees from right to left Zephyr (wind) chasing a nymph about a forest. From their eventual union Flora the goddess of flowers is born, and she is depicted scattering flowers from her lap. Farther back Venus is standing in the middle of an orange grove while Cupid flies above her shooting one of his arrows. Farther left are the three Graces dancing with their fingers entwined. At the far left, Mercury waves away the clouds from the orchard with a gesture of his hand.

Birth of Venus is a large oil painting on canvas, nine feet by five and a half feet, divided into three panels. The center panel represents the goddess Venus who is emerging from the ocean on a shell, blown by the winds from the left while on the right, the goddesses of the seasons are handing her a flowered cloak.

Directions: The Villa di Castello is on the outskirts of Florence, about three and a half miles southwest toward the city of Petraia.

Raphael

Raphael was born Raffaello Sanzio in the Italian city of Urbino in 1483, moved to Florence in 1504, and remained there until

1508. During his brief stay in Florence, Raphael had the opportunity of studying with the city's most illustrious masters, da Vinci and Michelangelo.

Raphael's genius is in his unique ability to synthesize the qualities of both da Vinci and Michelangelo to create a form of painting that captured the dramatic and rich qualities of da Vinci and the sculpturally solid figures associated with Michelangelo.

Raphael remained in Florence for only four years, and therefore very few of his paintings are in the city. Fortunately, however, visitors can see one of the many works he painted of Mary in the church of San Lorenzo, just two blocks from the Duomo.

Madonna of the Goldfinch

This picture (see p. 47), painted in 1506 for Lorenzo Nasi, depicts the Virgin Mary as a loving mother who has just stopped reading to watch the game of the young St. John who is holding a goldfinch that Jesus is touching. The influence of da Vinci can be seen in the pyramidal positioning of the figures as well as in the sfumato, the hazy landscape. The influence of Michelangelo is evident in the rendering of the bodies— all are slightly large, and the knees in particular have the heavy knobby quality of Michelangelo's work. Unique to Raphael's painting is the gentleness of the three faces and the lighthearted laugh on the face of St. John as he watches Jesus stroke the goldfinch. This sort of playfulness has never been seen before in Florentine art.

Directions: The Church of San Lorenzo is just two blocks due north of the Duomo.

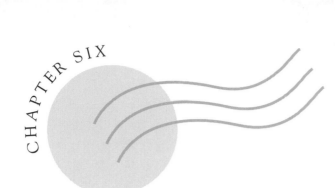

CHAPTER SIX

Casual Sightseeing

E ven the most ardent art lovers who come to Florence sometimes need diversion from its unrivaled collection of sculpture, paintings, and architecture. The city has many other activities and sights to offer visitors. A day wandering four of the city's unique piazzas or four of the beautiful bridges spanning the Arno offers an opportunity to relax and do a little shopping.

Riders parade their horses in a circle in the Piazza Santa Croce.

Girolama Savanarola

Tourists by the thousands travel to Florence to enjoy the riches of the city in the forms of its paintings, sculptures, and magnificent architecture. Most of these artistic riches were paid for by the church and wealthy families.

Not everyone was favorably impressed with this lavish display of wealth. When he arrived in Florence, in the mid-1480s, Girolamo Savanarola, a Dominican monk began denouncing what he perceived to be a decadent, corrupt, and immoral society. Specifically, he denounced the banking families and all of the great patrons of the arts—even the pope.

Savonarola took his pulpit and began delivering sermons warning the citizens of Florence against the evils of excessive wealth. He even went so far as to predict that Lorenzo de' Medici and other wealthy bankers would die early deaths if they did not give up their wealth to the poor. Savonarola went beyond his attack against avarice to demand that the Medici family give up its political dominance over the city.

Savonarola had some success. Money for relief was raised and given to the starving population, shops were opened to give work to the unemployed, a bank was established for charitable loans, and taxes on the poor were reduced.

The majority of the Florentines and all of the wealthy families finally turned on Savonarola. On May 23, 1498, the bishop of Florence stripped Savonarola of his priestly garb, excommunicated him—even though he did not posses the authority to do so—and ordered him hanged with two other men and then burned. The gallows were built in the Piazza della Signoria and the sentence was carried out before a crowd that gathered to witness the execution.

Four Great Piazzas

In Italy, the piazzas are the centers of life in each city, and Florence is blessed with many of them in every quarter. Each piazza is a large public square where people meet to shop, visit with friends, family, and neighbors, get haircuts, gossip, negotiate business deals, enjoy holiday festivities, play with their children, and take time out from their busy schedules for a bite to eat.

Each piazza in the city has a unique spirit. Travelers to Florence will enjoy the four recommended below for their contributions to the culture and character of the city. These four piazzas are conveniently located in the center of the city and are "must see" attractions on anyone's itinerary.

Piazza della Signoria

The Piazza della Signoria has been the political heart of the city for the past 250 years. This piazza began taking shape around 1250 when about forty houses and defense towers were torn down to clear the large area. This explains the unusual irregularity of the square and why the buildings around it are unaligned, unlike those around most of the other piazzas in the city.

This piazza takes its name from the most important monument bordering it, the Palazzo della Signoria designed by Arnolfo di Cambio as the city's town hall. Over the years the piazza has become an art center where several of the city's most important major sculptures are on display, including Michaelangelo's *David*, Donatello's *Judith and Holofernes*, and an equestrian statue of Cosimo de' Medici by Giambologna.

This square also has great historical importance as the place where many criminals have been executed, the most famous of whom was the monk Savonarola who was hanged and whose body was burned in 1498. Equally interesting are a few remains of Roman Florence that have been discovered underneath many of the houses surrounding the piazza. These include some Roman baths and a workshop for the dyeing of cloth.

Piazza Santa Croce

Just three blocks north of the Piazza della Signoria visitors will find the Piazza Santa Croce, the piazza for sports fans. The huge rectangular space, found in front of the Franciscan Church of Santa Croce, is large enough to accommodate large crowds. For this reason, it is the site of celebrations such as Carnival and May Day

festivities as well as the athletic tournaments of jousting and a football game that is especially popular with young members of the Florentine aristocracy.

This piazza evolved over a hundred-year period beginning in the thirteenth-century when many of the old buildings were torn down leaving only a few around the perimeter. The two most famous palaces facing the piazza are the fourteenth-century Palazzo Cocchi-Serristori and, at the opposite end of the piazza, the Palazzo dell' Antella, which belonged to the Cerchi family.

In addition to sporting events, the Piazza Santa Croce has a history of use for important civic and religious events. This is where the Franciscan preachers, as well as Santo Bernardino of Siena, addressed the population in times of despair such as when the Black Plague devastated the city's population in 1348.

Piazza del Duomo

Small in comparison to many of the other piazzas in Florence, the Piazza del Duomo is the religious center of the city. Situated between the Duomo and the Baptistery, this small piazza was once used as a cemetery. It is interesting to note that this early Christian complex was built near the northeastern limits of the original Roman camp.

If tourists to Florence arrive on June 24 to celebrate the feast day of St. John the Baptist, the patron saint of Florence, they will enjoy watching the ceremony that takes place in the Piazza del Duomo.

Traditional Football

If visitors to Florence enjoy a brutal ball game called *Giuoco del Calcio*, they might consider visiting during the Carnival season or on the feast of St. John when this football game is played. The football games are played in the Piazza Santa Croce as they have been for more than one hundred years.

The games begin with opening ceremonies led by members of the aristocracy followed by the *gonfalonieri* of the four city quarters, then by flag wavers, mace bearers, musicians, and the referee. Last of all, the players enter dressed in the traditional colors of the four quarters: blue for Santa Croce, green for San Giovanni, red for Santa Maria Novella, and white for Santo Spirito.

The game is held in the center of the Piazza Santa Croce, which is covered in sand for the occasion to protect the players. Two teams play at a time and the objective of the game is to push, kick, or throw a round leather ball past their opponent's end line into a net. Each team consists of twenty-seven players who kick, bite, shove, elbow, and punch each other to move the ball. By the end of a game, many players leave the piazza with bloody noses and missing teeth. The team that beats all of its opponents wins a calf, which is slaughtered and eaten as part of the victor's celebration.

The game is rich in history. Once, while the city was besieged by the Spanish army, the population assembled as usual to watch the traditional game. The match took place before the eyes and under the cannon fire of the enemy. Following the games, the Florentines went back to defending their city.

Visitors will cheer while watching an exciting football game in the Piazza Santa Croce.

Residents of Florence enjoy a stroll through the Piazza del Duomo, the city's religious center.

The festivities begin with the covering of this relatively small piazza with a set of blue canopies painted with silver stars. Following a procession carrying sacred relics from the Duomo is the show everyone waits for. A band of men pulling St. John's cart enters the piazza where the cart is ceremoniously set on fire. This is one of the most electrifying festivals celebrated in the city and it culminates with a massive fireworks display.

Visiting religious dignitaries from Rome, including the pope, take part in a procession along with Florence's most prominent families. Amid the fluttering of the colorful banners from the city's four districts, the single-file procession zigzags back and forth between the Duomo and the Baptistery.

Even if religious visitors cannot coordinate their schedules to enjoy the cere-mony of a papal visit, they will enjoy seeing the Column of St. Zanobus that stands near the north door of the Baptistery. This well-known column was erected in 1384 to mark the site of a dead elm tree, which is said to have sprung to life when the coffin containing the body of the bishop Zanobus bumped into it while being carried to its resting place.

Piazza Mercato Vecchio

The Piazza Mercato Vecchio (Old Market Place) is the place to go to find just about anything that anyone could want to buy. This teeming open-air market is also the most colorful, energetic, and congested of all the piazzas. All citizens of Florence must come here to buy their daily food, so visitors will see every type of dress from motley peasant costumes to the elegant attire of aristocrats. Located at the geographical center of Florence, this piazza is also the commercial center of all of Tuscany.

Each morning, temporary tents and stalls are erected to sell clothes, tools, medical supplies, kitchenware, pottery, flowers, meats, cheeses, breads, fish, fruits, nuts, onions, garlic, spices, pies, and the skins and heads of farm animals. Even exotic animals such as hawks, falcons, pheasant, and wild boar can be found in the marketplace. The selling day lasts from dawn to dusk amid the constant clamor of sellers calling out their products and buyers haggling to bring down the prices.

The Mercato Vecchio is also one of the best places for observing peoples' habits. Through the congestion of a thousand or more people elegant wealthy women are carried from stall to stall each seated in a litter borne on the shoulders of four men while prostitutes, who by law must wear gloves on their hands and bells on their

Life in the Mercato Vecchio

Of all of the marketplaces in Florence, the Mercato Vecchio has always been the largest and most frequented, providing the largest selection of goods. The Florentine poet Antonio Pucci, who loves the Mercato Vecchio, *captures the pulse and excitement of the market in this poem:*

Craftsmen and dealers of all sorts have stands
Stocked with all kinds of things. . . .
Wool and cloth dealers abound;
Apothecaries and grocers put their wares on show;
Traders in pots and pitchers can be found. . . .
Near by stand massive vaults, where goods are stored,
And splendid butchers' stalls where they display
What are the primest cuts in Florence we're assured . . . .
And when the time comes for fruit to be sold at fairs
Girls from the country pack their baskets high
With ripe round figs and grapes, peaches and pears.
If you try to repartee with them, they won't be shy,
And some of them, brighter than florins shine,
With flowers from gardens that they tend nearby.
No garden, though, ever looked half as fine
As the Mercato Vecchio does when spring is here.
It feeds the eye and taste of every Florentine.
And in this world it can't be matched—that's clear.

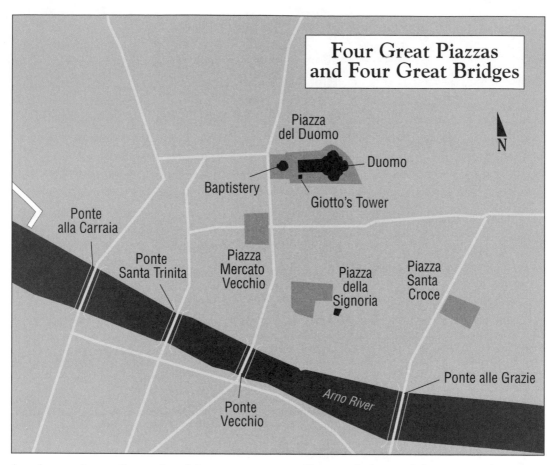

Four Great Piazzas and Four Great Bridges

Piazza del Duomo

Duomo

Baptistery

Giotto's Tower

N

Ponte alla Carraia

Ponte Santa Trinita

Piazza Mercato Vecchio

Piazza della Signoria

Piazza Santa Croce

Ponte alle Grazie

Arno River

Ponte Vecchio

heads, wander in the midst of the commotion. Beggars, always on the lookout for an opportunity to snatch a piece of fruit or cheese jostle the crowds side by side with pickpockets trying to snatch a coin or two for a bite to eat while heralds responsible for making public announcements ride through the throng on horseback calling out the news of the day. By sunset, all tents and stalls are disassembled and stored away until the next morning.

If solitude appears more attractive than the congestion of the piazzas, a quiet stroll over the city's four bridges will provide beautiful vistas and time to relax.

Four Great Bridges

The Arno River that snakes its way to the coast of the Ligurian Sea flows through Florence dividing it into two unequal parts. The river flows from east to west dividing Florence into the *Centro Storico* (historic center) to the north and the less crowded *Oltrarno* over the Arno to the south. When the city was small, it was contained on the north side of the river but over the years as the city grew in size and stature, many new homes and manufacturing buildings were located across the river. This expansion necessitated bridges to carry the traffic.

Linking the two areas of the city are, from south to north, the Ponte alle Grazie, Ponte Vecchio, Ponte Santa Trinita, and the Ponte alla Carraia. Since these four bridges are within easy walking distance of each other, many visitors make an excursion of crossing all four of them in one day while enjoying their shops as well as the beauty of the river.

Ponte alle Grazie

The Ponte alle Grazie, the Bridge of the Graces, was built in 1237. Of the four bridges, this one was the third built and is the only one that survived the great flood of 1333. The bridge was originally called Ponte Rubaconte, after the city official, Rubaconte da Mandello, and subsequently renamed Ponte alle Grazie, after the Church of Santa Maria delle Grazie. Unique to this bridge are the two small white convent houses at either end. From time to time, merchants have built small wooden shops to sell their wares to foot traffic.

Ponte Santa Trinita _pre Hest_

Of all of the bridges that cross the Arno, Florentines agree that Ponte Santa Trinita is the most beautiful with its graceful arching lines. The last of the four bridges, it was completed in 1252. Initially built of wood, it collapsed after only seven years and was replaced by a stone bridge, which lasted until the flood of 1333. It was subsequently replaced with the five-arch bridge designed by Taddeo Gaddi that visitors see today.

Ponte Santa Trinita became a necessity when the left bank became more important to the city as a result of the ducal residence being built there. The major adjoining street, Via Maggio, one of the most traveled streets in town, connects to the Ponte Santa Trinita.

Ponte Vecchio

The Ponte Vecchio (Old Bridge) is the oldest in Florence as well as everyone's favorite. The bridge was initially constructed of wood in 972 at the narrowest point of the Arno River. During the winter of 1177 heavy rain and a surging river undermined the support and toppled it into the river. It was replaced by a stone

A view from the Ponte Vecchio with the Duomo in the background.

bridge but in 1333, once again, winter flooding tore it apart sending it downstream beneath the raging cold water. The bridge visitors see today was built nearly two hundred years ago in 1345.

Compared to the other bridges spanning the river, the Ponte Vecchio is unique in its construction and aesthetic appeal. Supported by two stone and concrete piers midstream, a concrete roadway connects the two banks. Unlike all other bridges along the Arno, this one has walls running its entire length that are covered by a tile roof providing merchants, shoppers, and pedestrians shelter from the rain and hot sun.

At the end of the fifteenth century as the population and tourist trade increased, Grand Duke Ferdinando de' Medici ordered the goldsmiths to replace the butchers as the permanent occupants of the bridge. The butchers had been slaughtering cattle on the bridge allowing blood to run into the river along with shovelfuls of inedible body parts. The wafting stink offended many who finally insisted the change be made.

Visitors walking along the riverbanks can see a row of small square windows along the top floor of the bridge. These windows illuminate a private corridor used by members of the Medici family to move about between their various residences without having to step into the streets and mix with the crowd.

In addition to housing Florentine goldsmiths, the bridge remains the preferred execution spot for hanging criminals.

Ponte alla Carraia

As commerce increased in twelfth-century Florence and manufacturing began to expand to the left bank of the Arno, the one bridge across the river, the Ponte Vecchio, was no longer capable of carrying all of the traffic. The second bridge was built downstream of the Ponte Vecchio and was simply called the Ponte Nuovo (New Bridge) when completed in 1220. It was subsequently renamed Ponte alla Carraia because of its proximity to Carraia Gate. Like on the Ponte Vecchio, many wood shacks have been built on the bridge to serve as shops for many of the city's craftsmen.

This bridge was originally built of wood but it was swept away by a flood in 1269 and later rebuilt. In 1274 it was again washed away by the fury of the Arno. Its most famous collapse, however, was not the result of flooding. In 1304, under the weight of the throngs watching a spectacle being performed on boats on the river, the bridge collapsed. It was rebuilt only to become a victim of the floods of 1333. Between 1334 and 1337, it was rebuilt following a design by Giotto, which then served as a model for the city's next two bridges.

For travelers who may be exhausted by the city's art and architectural treasures, Florence also offers many of the finest shops where tourists can buy the best quality and latest fashions to take home with them.

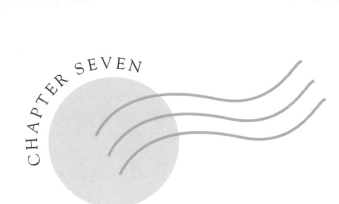

CHAPTER SEVEN

Shopping

Florentines for generations have celebrated their city for providing the best shopping of any city in Europe; better than Rome, Paris, or London. Although Florence is not one of the great seaports, nonetheless the finest wares from Italy and around the world find their way to it. Merchants ship their products here because of the city's wealthy families who demand the finest goods money can buy and because the population of Florence, about ninety thousand, is the fifth largest in Europe.

Florentine merchants and business owners are able to serve everyone's needs with 33 banks, 120 clothing shops, 84 cabinetmaker shops, 54 marble-worker shops, 44 goldsmiths, 30 gold beaters and silver-wire makers, 66 apothecaries, 70 butchers, 8 fowl and game shops, and 23 wine shops.

Jewelry
The Ponte Vecchio is the official place of business for the city's best goldsmiths and jewelers. About fifty years ago, the rows of small wood houses set on each side of the bridge became home to forty-four goldsmiths. These craftspeople still practice the same gold and jewelry techniques

Like other European merchants this southern Italian gentleman contributes a wealth of goods to Florence.

pioneered by some of the city's most famous artists, many of whom such as Brunelleschi, Ghiberti, and Donatello later became legendary masters of sculpture, art, and architecture.

Located a short walk from the Palazzo di Pitti, the Ponte Vecchio is the most popular and most beautiful bridge that spans the river. The many jewelry shops are the wooden boxlike buildings that hang on the outsides of the bridge itself. To get to the shops, visitors walk along the bridge's span looking into the fronts of the shops as they stroll.

Favorite gold jewelry designs for women are various types of bands, clips for hair and clothing, and sculptural pendants adorned with irregular pearls, enameling, and colored gems. Also popular are brooches or pendants containing a miniature portrait, many styles of necklaces, and gold chains. As is the case with other cities, some goldsmiths are reputable and some are not. If shoppers are not able to determine the purity of the gold they are buying by comparing it to the weight of one of the gold florins in their purses, they are better off avoiding gold jewelry in favor of silver.

Clothes

Florence is the clothing capital of Europe. With roughly one-third of the city's residents employed by the wool trade, items of clothing are one of the travelers' best buys. Florence produces seventy thousand bolts of wool annually. Cloth and clothing last year generated more than 1.2 million florins in revenue. What tourists wish to buy will determine where to go in the city and the price to be paid.

Almost every building along any of the three major piazzas, the Old Market, the Duomo, and the Piazza della Signoria, will have bargains to be found. In addition to the piazzas, shoppers looking for the finest wool clothing have 270 shops to visit and for those looking for splendid silk clothing, the city has 83 shops open to the public. In addition to their wools and silks, local shops also carry an exceptional array of velvet, brocade, damask, taffeta, and satin. Because most of these clothes are made here in Florence, the prices are much more favorable to shoppers than in Rome, Naples, or Paris.

The best streets to wander while shopping for woolen goods are the Corso dei Tintori (Road of the Dyers) and Corso Cauldrini (Road of Cauldrons). Whichever of these streets shoppers visit, they will see clothing dangling from every possible overhang along the sidewalks. The scene walking along the clothing boulevards is a splash of colors with proprietors yelling out sale prices to entice novice buyers. Be prepared to be pulled into shops.

The most popular women's dress in Florence this year, which is available in almost every shop, is the *lucco*, an ankle-length gown with buttons down the front and a hood hanging down the back. Hoods are fashionable because the current style of women's long hair cannot fit under small hats or caps, which were popular several years ago when hairstyles were shorter.

For women of high fashion, several shops near the Piazza della Signoria specialize in dresses for those unconstrained by budget. Many colors of satin and velvet sewn with pearls and precious jewels are available. Some dresses have long trains that require assistants to keep them from dragging on the ground while others feature elegant wide sleeves. During the winter months, long dresses for the ultra-rich are trimmed in mink or ermine.

Clothing shops also cater to men. Leather or wool tunics can be purchased, as well as many colors of tights. During the winter, long coats or cloaks are worn. The latest styles, including some that are fairly outrageous, can be found. According to the Florentine writer Giovanni Villani, "Young men are more ostentatious with tunics growing shorter and shorter, legs displayed in highly colored hose, that go right up to the groin, codpieces boldly prominent."[7] Men can also purchase leather pouches to hold their money and other personal items.

If courageous shoppers are willing to venture away from the beaten tourist paths and wander the streets bordering the river, they will enjoy a special sight not seen by most visitors. On these streets, shoppers can purchase yardage to make

their own clothes. Houses here are fitted with iron brackets supporting wood bars from which colorful lengths of cloth hang and dance in the breeze like festival banners. As one of our writers describes the city, "Florence appears to be one vast drying and stretching ground. Cloth of all kinds and colors waves in great lengths in every quarter, which imports an extraordinary sight to the streets."[8]

Ladies can purchase dresses made of rich fabrics that are detailed with beads and jewels.

Suits of Armor

One of the best bargains found in Florence is a good suit of armor. All of the best armor makers are located in the San Giovanni quarter northeast of the cathedral. Whether shoppers are looking for battle armor, tournament armor, or ceremonial armor, the armor makers of Florence are famous throughout Europe for their design

Suits of armor, like those shown in this battle scene, can be purchased in the Piazza del Duomo.

and construction. Buyers can choose intricate designs on traditional armor that emphasize vertical lines and spiky silhouette designs or the modern designs of rounded and fluted surfaces like corrugated iron.

When purchasing a suit of battle armor, the purchaser is advised to pay particular attention to the construction of the suit especially as it pertains to the weight. Battle armor is meant to give maximum protection with minimal weight. A full suit of battle armor should not exceed about sixty-five pounds. Such a suit should be fitted close to the body to provide easy movement of the arms and legs and for mounting a horse, swinging a sword, and running. It is also important to be able to remove one's armor without assistance in the event that the wearer falls into a river during a battle.

If tournament armor is needed for competitive jousting and sword fighting, the weight of the suit should be twice that of battle armor—safety is of far greater importance than mobility. Never pay more for a suit of tournament armor than necessary because the vanquished warrior in a tournament is often required to give up his armor to the victor.

Shoppers looking for an exquisite suit of ceremonial armor should be prepared to spend a lot of money. Since these suits are intended for ceremonies and parades, their primary function is to serve as status symbols for their wearers. This sort of armor is decorated with etchings, gilding—

Custom-Made Armor

A good suit of armor must be custom made to precisely fit the wearer's body parts. Too small or too large and the armor is useless. At the heart of a good suit of armor are the plates of steel that are shaped to the contours of the warrior. There are three types of plates: flank plates, stomach plates, and chest plates (left, right, middle).

Flank plates should cover the distance from just above the point of the hip to approximately two inches below the armpit where the arm intersects the body. The idea is to get the maximum length that will still not bind arm movement or cut into the waist when the body bends. The number of flank plates varies, ranging from four to fourteen plates, three to seven inches wide. In most Florentine shops, tailors use fourteen plates, although the number used is strictly up to the individual. More plates make the armor look better because it has more shiny rivets on the outside, and it provides somewhat better protection. However, this obviously means a more costly suit because there are more plates to cut and more rivets to set.

The stomach plates are three inches wide, slightly wider if you have a long torso. The bottom plate may be made wider to provide more protection for the lower body. These plates should be about eleven inches long and almost, but not quite, reach the points of the hips.

Chest plates should be approximately eight by three inches in size with slight bulges extending from the bottom of the left and right plates for additional breast protection.

The maker of the armor will demand a down payment for the suit and the balance upon delivery.

---

a rustproofing technique—and highly embossed plates depicting scenes from the wearer's military exploits. The more money one is willing to spend, the more the elaborate armor becomes a piece of body jewelry.

The shops of master artists and their apprentices can be found on many small back streets of the city. Most are located near the Piazza del Duomo where the sounds of sculptors hammering bronze or chipping marble and the smell of oil-base paints attract the attention of shoppers. Inside art galleries, shoppers will generally find several apprentices making their own paint colors by grinding and mixing minerals, berries, flowers, insects, metal oxides, and scores of other materials for richly colored pigments.

Some master artists will paint your portrait, others specialize in street scenes of Florence or biblical scenes. Most paintings are executed on pieces of wood, which makes carrying the painting home

Local artists will paint portraits of various sizes that can be taken home as souvenirs.

Connoisseurs of art must understand that great artists the caliber of Giotto, Michelangelo, Verrocchio, Donatello, or da Vinci are not likely to be enticed away from their work for the pope and the wealthy families of Florence and Milan.

Slaves

Slaves, both girls and boys from Greece, Russia, and Turkey can be purchased at the Piazza Mercato Vecchio. If travelers wish to purchase a slave as a helper, the local Florentines recommend buying Tatars, those from eastern Turkey. They are cheap and are considered reliable and conscientious. Since slaves are chattel, the local law permits owners to "hold, sell, alienate, exchange, enjoy, dispose of by will and do with in perpetuity whatsoever they like with them."[9]

Slaves are prevented by law from wearing colorful clothing of any kind, especially colorful coats or dresses. As for shoes, they are only to wear wooden ones and if they wear any sort of hat, it must be nothing more than a linen towel. Owners of slaves, especially owners of Tatars, must be wary at all times of their well-known bizarre and sometimes violent behavior as well as their peculiar religious beliefs and rituals. In spite of certain liabilities, most slaves blend in well with the life of the city. Slave owners are encouraged to treat them humanely, to allow them to live with the family, and if they are good workers, to grant them their freedom with a pension before their death.

fairly safe although travelers on foot will find them quite heavy. Prices are determined by size, number of colors, and the artist's expertise. For travelers on a tight budget, traveling paintings, miniature works two to three inches square intended to be carried at all times by travelers, are the best bargain.

Many artists who specialize in frescoes can be commissioned here in the city and they will then come to your home to execute the work. Negotiations will include the size, composition, and price of the fresco as well as travel expenses and food and lodging while the work is being done.

CHAPTER EIGHT

Festivals and Events

F estivals, both religious and secular, add a great deal of color and drama to the life of Florence. These ceremonies and festivals, as many as forty a year, are carefully choreographed events that are sponsored by the city. They serve the dual purposes of maintaining age-old traditions that inspire patriotism and provide the commoners with much-needed entertainment in their otherwise drab lives. Visitors who are able to attend any of the festivals will leave the city with a better understanding of what makes Florence unique.

Religious Festivals

Religious holidays celebrated in Florence are numerous, easily one a month. Most of these holidays are celebrated according to the church calendar, which sets the days for such celebrations as Easter, Christmas, Lent, Ash Wednesday, Epiphany, and Pentecost.

One of the high points of the religious festival season, unique to Florence, is the June 24 Feast of St. John the Baptist, the patron saint of Florence. If visitors are able to arrange their travels to attend this celebration, it will be one of the highlights of their visit.

The celebration begins the night before with a procession through the streets led by religious officials carrying church relics that are kept in the Duomo. Here in Florence, the church owns seven of the thorns from Jesus' crown of thorns, three splinters from the cross, one of the nails of the cross, and one link from the chains that once restrained Jesus. These relics are carried to the Baptistery by the bishop as civic dignitaries representing the sixteen *granfaloni* follow behind carrying wax candles.

On June 24 all workshops are closed and decorated with banners and wreaths of flowers. Everyone turns out for the parade of floats that passes through the

Florentines parade colorful banners in the Festival of Gifts, one of several festivals celebrated in the Piazza della Signoria.

Piazza della Signoria with as many as twenty thousand candles carried by those taking part. Blue cloth canopies cover many of the other piazzas that are decorated with yellow lilies. Floats decorated with symbols of Florentine history are pulled through the city followed by riderless horses stampeding through the streets with spiked balls hanging from their sides. Later in the afternoon following the midday meal, a reckless horse race is run through the city with the victor receiving the prize of the *palio*, a colorful banner on a pole.

May Day Festival

The May Day festival is the favorite of all festivals in Florence. On this day visitors will see millions of flowers decorating the city in celebration of the coming spring.

Early in the morning, families depart from the city gates for the countryside that is in full bloom. Picnic baskets full of food are laid out in the grassy meadows and family members dance to the rhythm of songs sung and clapped. After lunch, armfuls of flowers are picked to decorate their horses and carts. The procession of hundreds of flower-laden carts returning to the city is wonderful to witness.

In the late afternoon, when fathers and mothers return home, the piazzas surge with youthful exuberance. Young men hang *maii* (branches of flowers sprinkled with sugared nuts and wrapped in blue ribbons) at the houses of their girlfriends. Then, in the evening, the streets and piazzas are choked with young men and women wandering back and forth while eyeing each other.

Tournaments

For sports-minded visitors, Florence has two popular events that can be seen nearly each weekend. The *Giuoco del Calcio* is a favorite spectator game played each Saturday in several of Florence's piazzas. This is a bloody sport in which two teams, often behaving like two unruly mobs, punch and kick one another while trying to run a leather ball past their opponent's goal line. At each end of the piazza the wealthy classes set up tents to shade them from the sun and to provide them with banquet facilities while watching the game. For visitors to Florence, however, there will be standing room only along the length of the piazza to watch this popular game.

A second popular sport is the horse race around the Piazza della Signoria

St. John's Cart

St. John's Cart, called the *Brindellone*, is a small cart that was originally used to carry a large candle in the procession from Piazza della Signoria to the Baptistery each June 24 to celebrate the feast day of St. John the Baptist. *Brindellone* means a small poor man, a word describing St. John the Baptist. The tradition is to explode the cart with harmless firecrackers at the end of the procession to the Baptistery.

The origin of this tradition began because of a Florentine nobleman, Pazzino de' Pazzi, the first crusader to scale the walls of Jerusalem in 1099. As a reward for his feat, he received two pieces of silica from the Holy Sepulchre. These flints were to ignite the cart and set off the firecrackers and small rockets.

Over the years this once simple cart has developed into a towering cart with a ten-foot base, thirty-three feet tall, thirteen feet wide, and divided into four tiers. Niches in the cart hold children, while a man dressed in skins to impersonate St. John, stands on the top. The man representing St. John is paid ten lire for his time plus all he can eat and drink while riding the cart. He also tosses coins to the crowd.

At the end of the procession, the entire city enjoys the fireworks when the cart is set on fire. Farmers believe it is a good omen for the coming harvest. The ceremony is very popular with tourists.

called the *Palio*, named after the colorful banner on a pole which is the victor's prize. This 1.25-mile race is run from the meadow near the Ognissanti to the finish line at San Pietro Maggiore twice a year; once on June 24 to celebrate St. John the Baptist, and again on August 15 to celebrate the Assumption of the Virgin Mary. It is well worth coming to Florence just for this race. Each of the sixteen districts of the city enters one horse and jockey.

The race begins with a colorful procession of the *palio* with about eleven hundred people wearing their traditional costumes. These people are divided into *Dame* (Ladies), *Cavalieri* (Lords), gon-falonieri (people carrying the banners with the symbol of their district), *musici* (musicians), and *sbandieratori* (people who perform traditional flag-waving routines).

Following the procession, the horses and riders enter the piazza to the shouts of thousands of spectators who line the route wagering on their favorites. At a shout from the race starter, the jockeys whip and kick their steeds while riding bareback around the slippery cobblestone course. Riders and their mounts often tumble over each other as they sprint around the tight turns to the finish line. Although the objective for the riders is to

A horse race is a fast-paced spectacle held on the Piazza della Signoria.

The clamor of lances against armor can be heard in a jousting tournament—a must-see for tourists in Florence.

win the *palio* along with fame and glory for their district, for the spectators, the sight of blood and broken bones is anticipated with more enthusiasm than is victory for the winning horse.

If visitors wish to see excitement without bloody carnage, Sunday afternoons at the Piazza Santa Croce draws large crowds for professional jousting. As has been the custom for about one hundred years, the objective is for two riders in full armor to charge each other at full speed to knock the opponent off his horse with a lance. The joust remains the last sporting event pitting one man against another.

For those seeking entertainment with no violence whatsoever, jousters on the Via Larga charge the shield of a dummy set on a swivel. If they strike the dummy with their lance, a whip attached to the dummy swivels around and lashes out at the rider who tries to avoid being hit.

Public Executions

For those who miss the *Giuoco del Calcio* and the *Palio* but still yearn for the sight of blood, public torture and executions occur sporadically and are announced by the town crier who calls out the event including the time and place. If visitors

The Joust

Before jousting became a popular sport, the activity was used to hone fighting skills on horseback during periods of peace. However, when peacetime became lengthy and the prospect of war grew dim, knights needed a way to retain their skills and make money at the same time.

The origins of jousting as a sport in Florence and other European cities dates back about one hundred years to the early 1400s. Jousts were restricted to nobility. Money was made by holding the loser for ransom and often taking his horses and armor as payment. The prospective combatants hang their armor and shields on the trees, tents, and pavilions around the arena for inspection to show that they are candidates, that they are worthy to fight, and that their shields and armor are valuable.

Although the object of the joust is to knock one's opponent off his horse, over time that feat has become increasingly difficult because the backs of the jousters' saddles are now a foot tall to keep them in the saddle. Now, a direct hit at full gallop will cause an opponent's death. Such deaths have led some rulers to ban tournaments using pointed lances that easily pierce armor in favor of blunted lances that might injure an opponent but not impale him. Some tournaments merely award points for hits and the competitor accumulating the most points is declared the winner. Although these "pleasure jousts" are popular, many Florentines still prefer jousts to the death.

Jousting sometimes draws thousands of spectators who sit in wooden stands and wager heavily on the riders. Women enjoy giving their favorite knight a scarf or a glove to show that he is their special warrior. Between the jousts, food and ale are consumed by the crowd.

miss the formal announcement of the execution, they may see the condemned being marshaled through the streets on the way to their place of death and are welcome to follow the crowd.

Florentine council members believe that public executions, witnessed by as many people as possible, deter crime. Consequently, citizens and visitors are encouraged to see what will happen to those who flaunt the laws of the city. Only recently, a slave girl by the name of Lucia, who poisoned her master, was burned at the stake.

Although some citizens are offended by public executions, some are indifferent and others enjoy the spectacle that sometimes attracts thousands of curious onlookers. Piero di Cosimo, goldsmith and local chronicler, took this rather favorable view of condemned criminals about to die:

A fair thing it is to go to the place of execution in the open air, while the multitude consoles you with sweet-meats and kindly words. You have a priest, the people pray for you, and you go to heaven with the angels. Lucky is the man who departs thus suddenly![10]

Although Florence is the financial heart and artistic soul of Tuscany, many other towns and cities have their own attractions well worth exploring by travelers. For those with time, many interesting smaller towns offer visitors sights and experiences that cannot be found in the more noisy, more expensive, and often more crowded city of Florence.

CHAPTER NINE

Around and About Tuscany

Following the Arno River west to the coast, travelers will find the delightful city of Pisa. Roughly fifty miles from Florence, Pisa sits ten miles inland from the Ligurian Sea in a broad verdant delta soaked by the meandering Arno River and high tides that inundate the coastal area. Although Florence and Pisa were once at war, both cities now coexist peacefully.

Pisa is one of the major port cities along the west coast of Italy, even though it sits inland from the sea. The deep harbor of the city provides safe moorings for large oceangoing freighters that arrive from other Italian ports as well as from

A trip to the port city of Pisa provides an enjoyable excursion outside of Florence.

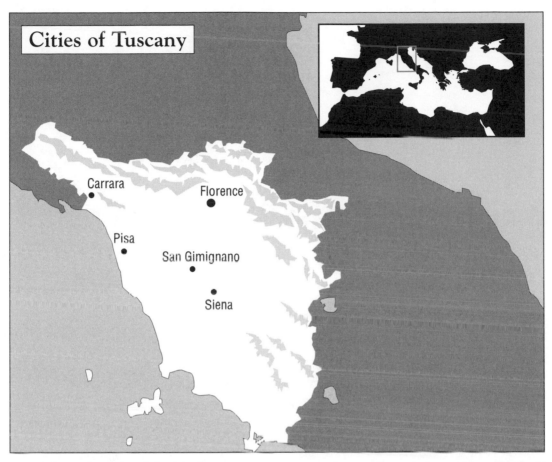

Cities of Tuscany

Carrara

Florence

Pisa

San Gimignano

Siena

ports along the rim of the Mediterranean Sea from Spain to the west, North Africa to the south, and Egypt, Damascus, Jerusalem, and Constantinople—recently renamed Istanbul—to the east. Freighters unload their products that are then dispersed throughout Tuscany on barges that negotiate the Arno and wagons that rattle over Tuscany's rutted roads.

The money made by merchants and traders in Pisa financed the city's main attractions, the three beautiful buildings located close together in the Piazza dei Miracoli (Plaza of Miracles). The first con-

structed was the city's main cathedral, Santa Maria, then the baptistery, and finally the bell tower. These three beautiful structures form a matched set of quintessential Pisan architecture. Of the three, the cathedral is the most famous and the most worthy of visitors' time.

The master builder Buschetto began the cathedral in 1063. It was consecrated in 1118 even though it was still years away from its completion around 1250. The cathedral is one of the finest in Tuscany, and although it is not as large as the cathedral in Florence, it is certainly as

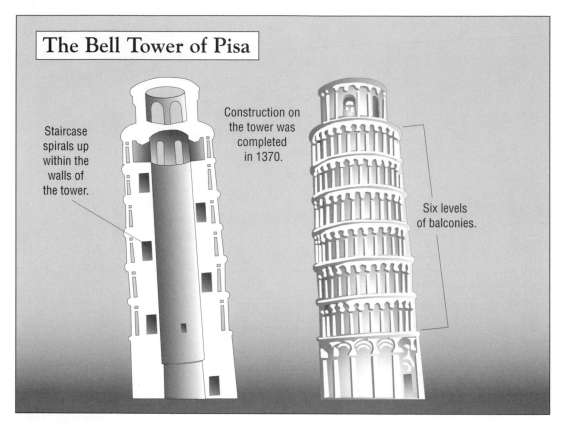

The Bell Tower of Pisa

Staircase spirals up within the walls of the tower.

Construction on the tower was completed in 1370.

Six levels of balconies.

beautiful. The visitor will enjoy its long rows of columns connected by arches and aisles and the interior that has an unusual timber roof. The exterior is covered in white Carrara marble with red bands, and the dome is elliptical. Although it is a relatively small cathedral, its unique beauty is derived from its beautiful proportions and the delicacy of its ornamental features.

The baptistery, similar to the one in Florence, is newer and more ornate. Construction began in 1152 and was completed in 1370 when the dome, covered with tiles and lead plaques and crowned by a bronze figure of St. John the Baptist, was added. Four elegantly sculpted marble doors depicting the life of St. John admit visitors inside.

The last building constructed in the Piazza dei Miracoli is the bell tower that was completed in 1370. It is cylindrical in shape, stands 193 feet tall, and has eight stories with open balconies that visitors can access from a spiral staircase. What makes the tower popular with tourists is the spectacular view of the piazza below and the distant hillsides from the top floor next to the bells.

The tower does have one odd characteristic that visitors have noticed for many years—a distinctive lean.

Carrara

Thirty-five miles up the coast north of Pisa is the small city of Carrara. Known for only one commodity, its beautiful white marble, the city is well worth visiting in spite of the fact that it cannot boast of any distinctive architecture, painters, or festivals. Its marble however, is the stone that covers more architectural treasures and is used to create more awe-inspiring statues than any other material. Despite Roman knowledge of Carrara's marble deposits, quarrying did not begin until the nearby cities were settled in the tenth century. A visit to this mountain of marble and a day watching the quarrying activities will never be forgotten.

Visitors approaching from the south will catch site of the mountain many miles before they arrive. Rising thousands of feet above the plain, the cuts that have been made by quarrymen for the past five hundred years have given the southwest side of the mountain a smooth white glacial appearance as if covered by snow.

Standing at the base of the mountain, spectators can see roads barely wide enough for donkey carts that zigzag upward to where the quarrymen work to break free large blocks of marble. The view is particularly electrifying when a large sheet of marble weighing hundreds of tons comes thundering down the mountainside and explodes into dozens of large chunks, millions of white chips, and a cloud of dust. The large usable pieces are then dragged or loaded on carts for cutting and polishing.

At the end of the day, visitors covered in white marble dust will welcome a dip in the water at one of the many beaches along the Ligurian Sea.

Winding paths on rocky terrain lead to the marble quarries of Carrara.

Siena

Thirty-five miles south of Florence is the beautiful city of Siena. Located in the Chianti hills, Siena is known for its rich artistic heritage, regional wines, and churches and architecture. Siena is divided into three parts, named after the city's three hills; San Martino, Citta, and Camolia. The road south from Florence is a major route and travelers will enjoy winding their way through the beautiful Chianti hills. Famed for its rich red soil, the entire city takes on a reddish hue from the roof tile and pottery manufactured and used here.

Although relatively small, Siena is architecturally and artistically one of Italy's richest cities. Visitors will enjoy wandering the city's neighborhoods within the walls that reveal enclosed narrow streets, eventually opening into the city's piazzas.

One of the more unusual institutions worth visiting is the University of Siena. Founded in 1240, it is the third oldest university in Italy. It consists of a school of law, a school of grammar, and a school of medicine. In 1252, the pope gave the university tax-free status allowing it to expand to the great size it has today. Visitors are welcome and should take the opportunity to visit its many buildings including the Casa della Sapienza (House of Wisdom) that combines classrooms

Visitors to Siena will appreciate the architecture of the Torre del Mangia with its red, brick façade and shimmering, white marble top.

The Black Death

The Black Death, correctly called the Bubonic Plague, swept all of Europe between 1348 and 1352 killing up to half the population of many cities including Florence, which saw its population decline from ninety thousand to fifty thousand.

Victims died a painful death with their bodies marked by grotesque swelling and dark blotches. Although the plague eventually disappeared, it continued to return on a smaller scale whenever sanitary conditions sank to low levels. For this reason, Florence spent a great deal of money building sewers and washing down streets daily to keep the city as free of vermin as possible. Other cities that did not have the sanitary conditions of Florence suffered even more.

Deaths became so common that the city sent carts around each morning to pick up dead bodies for burial in common ditches outside the walls of the city. The Italian writer Giovanni Boccaccio lived in Florence during the Black Death and in his book, the Decameron, *he grimly reported the treatment that victims received:*

It was the common practice of most neighbors, moved to less by fear of contamination by the putrefying bodies than by charity towards the deceased, to drag the corpses out of the houses with their own hands . . . and to lay them in front of the doors.

and student housing. Today, the price of residence for scholars is fifty gold florins a year for room and board.

The city's architectural jewel that all travelers should visit before moving on is the Palazzo Publico (Public Palace) constructed around 1350, which contains the tallest tower in the city, a 330-foot-tall bell tower. The Sienese refer to the tower as the *Torre del Mangia* (Tower of Eating), a reference to its chiming of the bells at lunchtime and dinnertime. Part of the beauty of the tower is that the bottom half is faced with Siena's famous red brick while the top is faced in gleaming white marble.

San Gimignano

Twenty miles south of Florence rises the city of San Gimignano on a 1,000-foot-high hill overlooking the Elsa Valley. The city takes its name from a tenth-century bishop who saved the village from barbarian hordes. The town increased in wealth during the next four hundred years because of the Via Francigena, the trading route that crossed through the Elsa Valley. Like most other Tuscan cities, San Gimignano fought wars against Florence but now both cities are at peace. Today the city is famed for its art treasures and more than seventy defense towers that still stand.

The 150-foot height of the Great Tower in the Piazza del Duomo of San Gimignano is sure to catch a visitor's eye.

The defense towers are the most pronounced architectural treasures of the city and can been seen for miles by approaching travelers. The towers, made of travertine (marble) and tufa (rock) blocks, stand between 100 and 150 feet tall and their construction dates back to the eleventh through thirteenth centuries. Even during the Black Plague between 1348 and 1352, families hid in the towers hoping to escape the agonizing disease. The towers of San Gimignano still stand as sentinels of the city in this isolated and poor region. Several of the rustic towers are open and visitors are encouraged to climb the stairs to the top to learn how they were built and to enjoy the view of the town and surrounding valley.

San Gimignano also has a cathedral, located in the Piazza del Duomo, that was dedicated in 1148. It is simple, befitting the poverty of the region. The front of the cathedral was erected in 1239 by Matteo Brunised who built two doors, one on the right for women and the other for men. Once inside, those who appreciate art will enjoy the cathedral's famous collection of frescoes. Of particular note are *The Old and the New Testament*, *The Last Judgment*, and *Stories of St. Fina*. Also well worth seeing is the fine collection of wood sculptures of the saints.

The other example of architecture worth seeing is the Palazzo del Popolo (People's Palace) that is surrounded by a wall and contains in the center a 150-foot defense tower named *The Great Tower*. Erected in 1300, this palace, which is today the home of the Town Council, is situated on the lefthand side of the Piazza del Duomo. In addition to its fascinating architecture, the palace has a rich collection of civic frescoes and paintings by many of the master painters dating back two hundred years.

Visitors who have had the opportunity to visit Florence and its many neighboring cities will understand why Tuscany is one of the world's most famous regions. Travelers cannot pass through this land without acquiring an awareness of its contributions to European history, its enchanting landscapes from the Apennines to the sea, its towns with museums and cathedrals, and its unparalleled contribution to the arts.

Notes

Chapter Three: Arriving in Florence, Where to Stay and Eat
1. Quoted in Charles L. Mee, *Daily Life in Renaissance Italy*. New York: American Heritage, 1975, p. 10.
2. Quoted in Christopher Hibbert, *Florence: The Biography of a City*. New York: W.W. Norton, 1993, p. 55.

Chapter Four: Architectural Monuments of Florence
3. L.B. Alberti, *On Painting*, trans. John Spencer. Florence: G.C. Sansoni, 1950, p.28.

Chapter Five: Finding the Masters
4. Giorgio Vasari, *Lives of the Artists*, trans. George Bull. Baltimore, MD: Penguin Books, 1967, p. 57.

5. Masaccio: The Life, The Genius, The Works. www.masaccio.it.
6. Quoted in Hibbert, *Florence: The Biography of a City*, p. 352.

Chapter Seven: Shopping
7. Quoted in Hibbert, *Florence: The Biography of a City*, p. 53.
8. Hibbert, *Florence: The Biography of a City*, p. 63.
9. Hibbert, *Florence: The Biography of a City*, p. 51.

Chapter Eight: Festivals and Events
10. J. Lucas-Dubreton, *Daily Life in Florence in the Time of the Medici*. New York: Macmillan, 1961, p. 137.

For Further Reading

Giovanni Boccaccio, *Decameron*. Trans. G.H. McWilliam. New York: Penguin, 1996. This book is one of the classics of the Italian Renaissance. It tells the story of ten young people who leave Florence to escape the Black Death of 1348 and organize their lives in the countryside through the pleasure and discipline of storytelling.

Giovanni della Casa, *Galateo: Of Manners and Behaviours in Familiar Conversation*. Trans. Robert Peterson. London: Prive Press, 1892. This is one of the more unusual books that provides an account of how people should behave in public. Della Casa lived and wrote during the early sixteenth century and he freely gives advice on all facets of public behavior.

D.V. Kent and F.W. Kent, *Neighbors and Neighborhoods in Renaissance Florence: The District of the Red Lion in the Fifteenth Century*. Locust Valley, N.Y.: J.J. Augustin, 1982. This is a highly academic account of the importance of the neighborhoods of Florence and their role in the politics and social life of the Florentines.

Pierre Leprohon, *Florence*. Trans. David Macrea. Geneva: Minerva, 1978. This is primarily a photo book containing both modern photographs as well as photographs of Renaissance paintings of Florence and its well-known architecture.

Richard Trexler, *Public Life in Renaissance Florence*. New York: Academic Press, 1980. This book describes the ritualistic ways that Florentines interacted with each other and foreigners and their divinities between the thirteenth and sixteenth centuries. Trexler emphasizes the importance of a wide variety of rituals in the lives of the Florentines.

Works Consulted

L.B. Alberti, *On Painting*. Trans. John Spencer. Florence: G.C. Sansoni, 1950. Written during the middle of the Renaissance, this work describes the history of painting and art including details on Donatello, Brunelleschi, and Ghiberti.

Gene Brucker, *Renaissance Florence*. New York: John Wiley & Sons, 1969. This is considered among scholars as one of the best works on Florence during the Renaissance.

Leonardo Bruni, *History of the Florentine People*. Trans. and ed. James Hankins. Cambridge, MA: Harvard Press, 2001. Bruni was a fifteenth-century traveler who came to Florence and fell in love with the city. He wrote his book to illustrate the many fine qualities of the city but in so doing, he tended to paint a suspiciously favorable picture of the city.

John Gage, *Life in Italy at the Time of the Medici*. New York: G.P. Putnam's Sons, 1968. Mr. Gage's book on fifteenth-century Italy has become a classic. He provides a wealth of information about the times and what it was like to live and work in cities throughout Italy.

Christopher Hibbert, *Florence: The Biography of a City*. New York: W.W. Norton, 1993. This is an excellent scholarly work describing the history of Florence from Roman times through 1992. Each chapter carries a theme highlighting the major political and social events of the time.

G.E. Kidder Smith, *Looking at Architecture*. New York: Harry N. Abrams, 1990. This book provides short discussions of many of the world's innovative buildings as well as some architectural drawings and photographs.

Luca Landucci, *A Florentine Diary from 1450 to 1516*. Trans. Alice de Rosen Jervis. New York: E.P. Dutton, 1927. The author of this work was a Florentine apothecary who wrote an extensive diary about the "noble and valiant" men of Florence. Included in the diary are insights into the way of life in Florence at the time.

J. Lucas-Dubreton, *Daily Life in Florence in the Time of the Medici*. New York: Macmillan, 1961. This book is an excellent account of Florence under the Medici. It covers many interesting aspects of the city's politics, social events, daily life, and history.

Charles L. Mee, *Daily Life in Renaissance Italy*. New York: American Heritage, 1975. This excellent book describes the Renaissance in Italy by themes in the lives of the people. Filled with art and well peppered with quotations, it paints a vivid picture of the times.

Giorgio Vasari, *Lives of the Artists*. Trans. George Bull. Baltimore, MD: Penguin Books, 1967. Vasari was a writer who lived in Florence when many of the artists lived and worked there. His biographical sketches of the artists, many of whom were his friends, are both insightful and amusing. The one drawback to Vasari's stories is that they tend to be excessive in their praise for each artist.

Website

Masaccio: The Life, The Genius, The Works (www.masaccio.it). This website provides an excellent abbreviated discussion of Masaccio and his paintings.

Index

Picture Credits

About the Author

James Barter is the author of more than a dozen nonfiction books for middle school students. He received his undergraduate degree in history and classics at the University of California Berkeley followed by graduate studies in ancient history and archaeology at the University of Pennsylvania. Mr. Barter has taught history as well as Latin and Greek.

A Fulbright scholar at the American Academy in Rome, Mr. Barter worked on archaeological sites in and around the city as well as on sites in the Naples area. Mr. Barter also has worked and traveled extensively in Greece.

Mr. Barter currently lives in Rancho Santa Fe, California, with his seventeen-year-old daughter, Kalista.